COACHES &
FITNESS
PROFESSIONALS

Ferguson
An imprint of ☑® Facts On File

Careers in Focus: Coaches & Fitness Professionals

Ferguson
An imprint of Facts On File, Inc.
132 West 31st Street
New York NY 10001

Careers in focus. Coaches & fitness professionals.
    p. cm.
Includes bibliographic references.
Contents: Aerobics instructors—Athletic directors—College sports coaches—Diet and
fitness writers—Dietitians and nutritionists—Fitness directors—Health club owners and
managers—Lifeguards and swimming instructors—Motivational speakers—Personal
trainers—Physical education teachers—Professional sports coaches—Recreational therapists—Sports instructors and coaches—Sports physicians—Sports psychologists—
Sports trainers—Yoga and pilates instructors.
    ISBN 0-8160-5548-3 (hc: alk. paper)
    1. Coaching (Athletics)—Vocational guidance—Juvenile literature. 2. Physical
education and training—Vocational guidance—Juvenile literature. [1. Coaching
(Athletics)—Vocational guidance. 2. Physical education and training—Vocational
guidance. 3. Sports—Vocational guidance. 4. Vocational guidance.] I. Title:
Coaches & fitness professionals. II. Title: Coaches and fitness professionals.
III. J.G. Ferguson Publishing Company.
    GV711.C33 2004
    796'.07'7023—dc22   2003017712

Table of Contents

Introduction

In today's fast-paced, computer-driven world, physical fitness is sometimes taken for granted, or worse, completely neglected. We have become more sedentary than our ancestors: For example, we drive to the supermarket or even McDonald's for dinner instead of hunting it down or growing our food in the wild. While we don't necessarily need (or want) to go back to our cave-dwelling roots, we do need to balance our society's tendency towards huge portions and fatty foods with exercise. To battle the "super-size-it" bulge and improve our physical endurance and health, we need to stay active.

The thousands of professionals in the sports and fitness industry help us do just that. Whether they are coaching a team of baseball players, leading an aerobics class, or encouraging young students in physical education class, coaches, sports trainers, and other fitness professionals make us fitter and more knowledgeable about the importance of exercise and diet in our daily lives. Rapid sales of weight-loss books and videos attest to our need for motivational help. The increased demand for physical trainers and group fitness instructors indicates our interest in getting fit and staying healthy. Increased attendance at sporting events shows our continued desire for athletic competition. Indeed, the sports and fitness industry shows no sign of decline and should continue to employ thousands of athletes, coaches, writers, instructors, and therapists in the coming years.

Each article in *Careers in Focus: Coaches & Fitness Professionals* discusses a particular sport or fitness occupation in detail. Some of the articles appear in Ferguson's *Encyclopedia of Careers and Vocational Guidance,* but have been updated and revised with the latest information from the U.S. Department of Labor, professional organizations, and other sources. In addition, the following new articles have been written specifically for this book: Athletic Directors, College Sports Coaches, Diet and Fitness Writers, Fitness Directors, Health Club Owners and Managers, Lifeguards and Swimming Instructors, Motivational Speakers, Physical Education Teachers, Professional Sports Coaches, and Yoga and Pilates Instructors.

The **Quick Facts** section provides a brief summary of the career including recommended school subjects, personal skills, work environment, minimum educational requirements, salary ranges, certification or licensing requirements, and employment outlook. This section also provides acronyms and identification numbers for the

I

following government classification indexes: the *Dictionary of Occupational Titles* (DOT), the Guide to Occupational Exploration (GOE), the National Occupational Classification (NOC) Index, and the Occupational Information Network (O*NET)-Standard Occupational Classification System (SOC) index. The DOT, GOE, and O*NET-SOC indexes have been created by the U.S. government; the NOC index is Canada's career classification system. Readers can use the identification numbers listed in the Quick Facts section to access further information about a career. Print editions of the DOT (*Dictionary of Occupational Titles.* Indianapolis, Ind.: JIST Works, 1991) and GOE (*The Complete Guide for Occupational Exploration.* Indianapolis, Ind.: JIST Works, 1993) are available at libraries. Electronic versions of the NOC (http://www23.hrdc-drhc.gc.ca) and O*NET-SOC (http://online.onetcenter.org) are available on the World Wide Web. When no DOT, GOE, NOC, or O*NET-SOC numbers are present, this means that the U.S. Department of Labor or Human Resources Development Canada have not created a numerical designation for this career. In this instance, you will see the acronym "N/A," or not available.

The **Overview** section is a brief introductory description of the duties and responsibilities involved in this career. Oftentimes, a career may have a variety of job titles. When this is the case, alternative career titles are presented.

The **History** section describes the history of the particular job as it relates to the overall development of its industry or field.

The **Job** describes the primary and secondary duties of the job.

Requirements discusses high school and postsecondary education and training requirements, any certification or licensing that is necessary, and other personal requirements for success in the job.

Exploring offers suggestions on how to gain experience in or knowledge of the particular job before making a firm educational and financial commitment. The focus is on what can be done while still in high school (or in the early years of college) to gain a better understanding of the job.

The **Employers** section gives an overview of typical places of employment for the job.

Starting Out discusses the best ways to land that first job, be it through the college placement office, newspaper ads, or personal contact.

The **Advancement** section describes what kind of career path to expect from the job and how to get there.

Earnings lists salary ranges and describes the typical fringe benefits.

The **Work Environment** section describes the typical surroundings and conditions of employment—whether indoors or outdoors, noisy or quiet, social or independent. Also discussed are typical hours worked, any seasonal fluctuations, and the stresses and strains of the job.

The **Outlook** section summarizes the job in terms of the general economy and industry projections. For the most part, Outlook information is obtained from the Bureau of Labor Statistics and is supplemented by information taken from professional associations. Job growth terms follow those used in the *Occupational Outlook Handbook*. Growth described as "much faster than the average" means an increase of 36 percent or more. Growth described as "faster than the average" means an increase of 21–35 percent. Growth described as "about as fast as the average" means an increase of 10–20 percent. Growth described as "more slowly than the average" means an increase of 3–9 percent. Growth described as "little or no change" means an increase of 0–2 percent. "Decline" means a decrease of 1 percent or more.

Each article ends with **For More Information**, which lists organizations that provide career information on training, education, internships, scholarships, and job placement.

Throughout the book you will also find also photos of some careers, informative sidebars, and interviews with professionals in the field.

If you have a love of fitness and exercise and a knack for working with others, a career in coaching or fitness may be right for you. Take the time to explore all of the careers in this book, and be sure to contact the various organizations for additional information.

Aerobics Instructors

QUICK FACTS

School Subjects
Health
Physical education
Theater/dance

Personal Skills
Helping/teaching
Leadership/management

Work Environment
Primarily indoors
Primarily one location

Minimum Education Level
High school diploma

Salary Range
$7.84/hour to $11.22/hour to
$26.06/hour

Certification or Licensing
Required for certain
positions

Outlook
Much faster than the average

DOT
153

GOE
10.02.02

NOC
5254

O*NET-SOC
39-9031.00

OVERVIEW

Aerobics instructors choreograph and teach aerobics classes of varying types. Classes are geared toward people with general good health as well as to specialized populations, including the elderly and those with specific health problems that affect their ability to exercise.

HISTORY

Physical fitness has only recently become an organized industry. As more people began to use exercise and weight training equipment, knowledgeable instructors were needed to teach beginners how to use the machines safely and effectively. Today, instructors' services usually are available to anyone who joins a health club.

Aerobics has also become widely respected by health professionals since it first became popular in the late 1970s and early 1980s, mainly because the importance of aerobic activity is now universally recognized. In addition, aerobics has diversified to include many options and levels of difficulty. Although the element of dance is still evident in some aerobic moves, it has been de-emphasized in many classes, primarily to encourage those who are less coordinated to participate. Instead of focusing on coordinated dance steps or complicated routines that are difficult to memorize, aerobic workouts now are more focused on a series of movements that aim to elevate the heart rate and work various muscle groups. For example, a particular class may seek to shape and tone specific muscle groups, such as the abdominals or hamstrings. This past decade has seen the introduction of several new branches of aerobics, including water aerobics, step aerobics, interval training, and interval circuit training.

Water aerobics is a popular form of low-impact aerobics. Impact refers to the stress placed on joints and bones during exercise. Because the water supports the body and creates resistance, it is an ideal exercise medium. Provided participants wear the proper safety equipment and are in the presence of others, they don't necessarily need to know how to swim, because in most classes, all the movements are done standing upright or holding onto the side of the pool. Water aerobics is especially well suited to older individuals because the water can be therapeutic for aching joints and muscles.

Another popular fitness class is step aerobics. In 1986, an aerobics instructor and body builder named Gin Miller developed a formal step training program after using the technique to recover from a knee injury. Basically, step aerobics involves the use of a specially designed stool or bench that sits from four to 12 inches off the ground. Participants step up and down in different patterns, which provides an excellent cardiovascular workout.

Another exercise trend is called interval training. In the late 1980s, Arlette Perry, an exercise physiologist with the University of Miami's Human Performance Laboratory, determined that alternating intense exercise movements with slower paced movements was better for aerobic fitness than a steady level of exercise, because it achieves higher heart rates. Interval classes today incorporate many different types of exercise to raise and maintain participants' heart rates, for example, blending high-impact aerobic moves with lower intensity exercises, such as marching in place or stretching.

Today, aerobics classes are often used in cross training, where amateur and professional athletes combine several different fitness activities to train for a certain sport. A popular workout is circuit training or interval circuit training, which combines aerobic exercise with weight lifting for a full body workout. In circuit training, the workout equipment is arranged to work one group of muscles at a time, alternating so that one set of muscles can rest while the next group is worked. As the individual moves through each piece of equipment in the circuit, the heart rate remains elevated, without the participants tiring as quickly as they would if repeating the same exercise.

New trends in fitness include aerobics classes for the whole family. Some daycare centers offer aerobics classes for kids that incorporate dancing or active playing to keep kids moving. Nursing

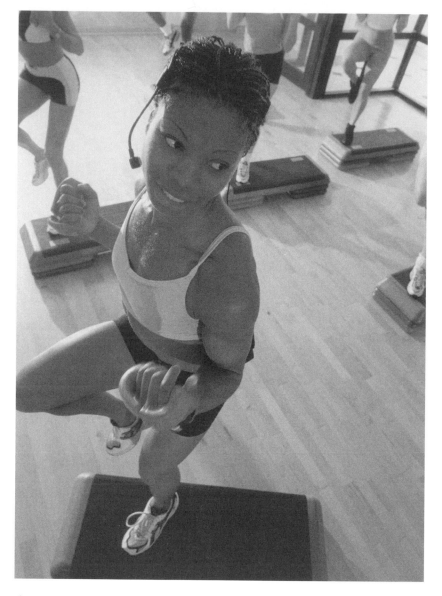

Aerobics instructors must be able to give verbal cues to class members while doing the exercise routine. *(Corbis)*

homes and assisted living complexes also offer aerobics to older individuals, adjusting exercise programs to the participants' abilities. For those who are wheelchair-bound or who have trouble standing up for longer periods, classes are held while members remain seated.

THE JOB

Three general levels of aerobics classes are recognized today: low impact, moderate, and high intensity. A typical class starts with warm-up exercises (slow stretching movements to loosen up muscles), followed by 35–40 minutes of nonstop activity to raise the heart rate, and ending with a cool-down period of stretching and slower movements. Instructors teach class members to monitor their heart rates and observe their bodies for signs of personal progress.

Aerobics instructors prepare activities prior to their classes. They choose exercises to work different muscles and put these movements to music during each phase of the program. Generally, instructors use upbeat music for the more intense exercise portion and more soothing music for the cool-down period. Instructors demonstrate each step of a sequence until the class can follow along. Additional sequences are added continuously as the class progresses, making up a longer routine that is set to music. Most classes are structured so that new participants can start any given class. The instructor either faces the rest of the room or faces a mirror in order to observe class progress and ensure that participants do exercises correctly.

Many aerobics instructors also lead toning and shaping classes. In these classes, the emphasis is not on aerobic activity but on working particular areas of the body. An instructor begins the class with a brief aerobic period followed by stretching and weight-bearing exercises that loosen and work major muscle groups.

Today, people have many options for exercising. Aerobic classes have grown in number and variety, from the traditional floor and step aerobics to introductory dance classes, such as hip-hop and ballet.

REQUIREMENTS

High School

Aerobics instructors should have a high school diploma. If you are interested in a fitness career, take courses in physical education, biology, and anatomy. In addition, be involved in sports, weight lifting, or dance activities to stay fit and learn to appreciate the value of exercise.

Postsecondary Training

Although it isn't always necessary, a college degree will make you more marketable in the fitness field. Typically, aerobics instructors do not need a college education to qualify for jobs; however, some employers may be more interested in candidates with a balance of ability and education. Essential college-level courses include anatomy, biomechanics, chemistry, first aid, health, kinesiology, nutrition, physics, physiology, psychology, and safety.

Certification or Licensing

Most serious aerobics instructors become certified. Certification is not required in most states, but most clients and fitness companies expect these professionals to have credentials to prove their worth.

Certifying agencies include the following: Aerobics and Fitness Association of America, American College of Sports Medicine, American Council on Exercise, and National Academy of Sports Medicine. Aerobics instructors should also be certified in cardiopulmonary resuscitation (CPR) before finding a job.

In addition, aerobics instructors are expected to keep up to date with the fitness field, becoming thoroughly familiar with the latest knowledge and safety practices. They should take continuing education courses and participate in seminars to keep their certification current.

Other Requirements

Aerobics instructors are expected to be physically fit, but are not expected to be specimens of human perfection. For example, members of an aerobics class geared to overweight people might feel more comfortable with a heavier instructor; a class geared towards the elderly may benefit from an older instructor.

EXPLORING

A visit to a health club, park district, or YMCA aerobics class is a good way to observe the work of aerobics instructors. Part-time or summer jobs are sometimes available for high school students in these facilities. It may also be possible to volunteer in a senior citizen center where aerobics classes are offered. If possible, enroll in an aerobics class to experience firsthand what a teaching job entails and to see what makes a good instructor.

"To explore this career, I recommend working part time in a gym or fitness facility," Tony Hinsberger, owner of Summit Fitness Personal Training, suggests. "Some clubs have an orientation position. People in this job take new members on a tour of the facility and show new members how to use the equipment safely. It typically doesn't require a degree, only on-site training."

Aerobics instructor workshops are taught to help prospective instructors gain experience. These are usually offered in adult education courses at such places as the YMCA. Unpaid apprenticeships are also a good way for future instructors to obtain supervised experience before teaching classes on their own. The facility may allow prospective aerobics instructors to take their training class for free if there is a possibility that they will work there in the future.

EMPLOYERS

Most aerobics instructors work for fitness centers and gymnasiums. Most employers are for-profit businesses, but some are community-based, such as the YMCA or a family center. Other job possibilities can be found in corporate fitness centers, colleges, retirement centers, and resorts. Some instructors work in more than one facility.

Most medium to large cities have one or more gyms or fitness centers; however, smaller towns may not have any such facilities. However, there may be limited openings at retirement homes, schools, and community centers in these small towns.

STARTING OUT

Students should use their schools' placement offices for information on available jobs. Often, facilities that provide training or internships will hire or provide job leads to individuals who have completed programs. Students can also find jobs through classified ads and by applying to health and fitness clubs, YMCAs, YWCAs, Jewish community centers, local schools, park districts, church groups, and other fitness organizations. Because exercise is understood to be a preventive measure for many health and medical problems, insurance companies often reward businesses that offer fitness facilities to their employees with lower insurance rates. As a result, students should consider nearby companies for prospective fitness instructor positions.

ADVANCEMENT

Experienced aerobics instructors can become instructor trainers, providing tips and insight on how to lead a class and what routines work well. A bachelor's degree in either sports physiology or exercise physiology is especially beneficial for those who want to advance to the position of health club director or to teach corporate wellness programs.

EARNINGS

Aerobics instructors are usually paid by the class and generally start out at about $10 per class. Experienced aerobics instructors can earn up to $50 or $60 per class. The U.S. Department of Labor reports that aerobics instructors and fitness trainers earned median hourly earnings of $11.22 in 2001. A majority of these workers earned between $7.84 and $18.06. Top instructors and trainers with experience earned $26.06 or more an hour.

A compensation survey by IDEA: The Health and Fitness Association reports that many employers offer health insurance and paid sick and vacation time to full-time employees. They also may provide discounts on products sold in the club (such as shoes, clothes, and equipment) and free memberships to use the facility.

WORK ENVIRONMENT

Most aerobics classes are held indoors. Depending on the popularity of the class and/or instructor, classes can get crowded and hectic at times. Instructors need to keep a level head and maintain a positive, outgoing personality in order to motivate people and keep them together. It is important that instructors make the class enjoyable yet challenging so that members will return class after class. They also need to be unaffected by complaints of class members—instructors need to realize that these complaints are not personal attacks. Despite dealing with occasional criticism, most aerobic instructors work with agreeable and pleasant participants and find it rewarding to help others achieve fitness goals.

OUTLOOK

Because of the country's ever-expanding interest in health and fitness, the U.S. Department of Labor predicts that the job outlook for aerobics instructors should remain very strong over the next several years. As the population ages, more opportunities will arise to work with the elderly in retirement homes. Large companies and corporations are also interested in keeping insurance costs down by hiring aerobics instructors to hold classes for their employees. America's often-touted "weight problem" will also have an effect on the popularity and demand for aerobics instructors. As communities, schools, and individuals attempt to shed the pounds, there will be a continuing need for fitness instructors and motivators.

FOR MORE INFORMATION

For information certification, contact
Aerobics and Fitness Association of America
15250 Ventura Boulevard, Suite 200
Sherman Oaks, CA 91403
Tel: 877-968-7263
Email: contactAFAA@afaa.com
http://www.afaa.com

For free information materials about sports medicine topics and information on certification, contact
American College of Sports Medicine
PO Box 1440
Indianapolis, IN 46206-1440
Tel: 317-637-9200
http://www.acsm.org

For more information about certification and careers in fitness, contact ACE.
American Council on Exercise (ACE)
1851 Paramount Drive
San Diego, CA 92123
Tel: 800-825-3636
http://www.acefitness.org

For fitness facts and articles, visit IDEA's website.
IDEA: The Health and Fitness Association
6190 Cornerstone Court East, #204
San Diego, CA 92121-3773
Tel: 800-999-4332
Email: nonmemberquestions@ideafit.com
http://www.ideafit.com

For information on certification, contact
National Academy of Sports Medicine
26632 Agoura Road
Calabasas, CA 91302
Tel: 800-460-6276
http://www.nasm.org

INTERVIEW

Jennifer Dixon is a group fitness instructor at Lincoln Park Athletic Club (LPAC) in Chicago. She has worked in the fitness industry for 16 years and was happy to talk about her experiences with the editors of Careers in Focus: Coaches & Fitness Professionals.

Q. What is the most important part of your job?

A. My primary job duty is to teach a safe, effective exercise class in accordance with the guidelines set forth by the American College of Sports Medicine (ACSM).

Q. Where do you work? Do you travel for your job?

A. I work for several health clubs in the city, mainly LPAC and Galter LifeCenter. I teach indoors in exercise studios and use my own transportation to get to each facility.

Q. How did you train for this job? What was your college major?

A. My college major was sociology with a minor in exercise science. My post-graduate degree is unrelated [to my current profession]. I became certified by the Aerobics and Fitness Association of America (AFAA) as an aerobics instructor (now called group fitness instructor) in 1992. I had to pass written and practical exams on exercise physiology, anatomy, kinesiology, safety guidelines, how to teach exercise, nutrition and weight management, personal training, business and leadership skills, mind/body connection, special populations, specialty classes, and training. These tests are based on guidelines set forth by the ACSM. I have also become certified as a personal trainer and perinatal fitness instructor, working with pregnant women and those who have recently given birth.

Q. Did your major prepare you for your career or, in retrospect, would you pursue another major? If so, what major?

A. My sociology major did not prepare me for this career, but my minor did—somewhat. In retrospect, I would have double-majored in a fitness field. I am considering pursuing a second master's degree in exercise science, anatomy, kinesiology, or another related field.

Q. Where did you get your first job? What did you do?

A. I started at Women's Workout World in Chicago in 1987. It was a good starting position because I was taught instructor skills and was slowly introduced to leading classes. Once I was teaching more regularly, I started giving club orientations to new members and designed exercise programs for individuals.

Q. What kind of sources are available to someone looking to get into this field?

A. There are many resources available online and in your local bookstore. The main thing is to get certified by any of the following: ACSM, AFAA, or the American Council on Exercise. These well-known certifying organizations host websites that offer information and study materials to prepare for your career and certification.

Q. What are the most important personal and professional qualities for fitness instructors?

A. While the most common qualification is a certification, a degree in the fitness field adds another level of credibility to your resume and allows you to demand higher pay. However, you can still make a decent amount of money with certification alone. It is important to look at the hiring trends in your city and state. For instance, in Chicago, you can make a substantial amount of money as an instructor, but in Washington, D.C., they pay almost 50 percent less for the same job—equivalent to what I made more than 10 years ago!

Q. What are some of the pros and cons of your career?

A. Pros: I enjoy helping people get fit, accomplish goals, feel better, and manage their physical problems. It's also a great job for getting to know a lot of people and having a flexible schedule. I sometimes teach for an hour at a time and then get to go home. I also have a free health club membership, get paid to exercise, and enjoy instructor discounts from Nike, Reebok, Adidas, New Balance, and other manufacturers.

Cons: I have to deal with aches and pains over time and sometimes just don't feel like teaching and motivating classes—let alone sweating! It also can be frustrating not to have back-to-back classes, especially if you have to travel a good distance to get to your job. And when not teaching as much, the pay isn't as good. Other occasional difficulties include finding a substitute teacher when I need one, feeling pressure to "pack'em in" for classes, and keeping up on the newest/trendiest exercises, such as Tae Bo.

Q. What is the most important piece of advice that you have to offer college students as they graduate and try to enter this field?

A. Get your degree and find your niche. You don't have to be on top of all the trends, just find what you like to do and do it well.

Athletic Directors

OVERVIEW

Athletic directors coordinate and oversee athletic programs at public and private colleges and universities. They manage staff; calculate budgets; negotiate broadcasting and other business contracts; raise funds to meet budget shortfalls; ensure that their programs meet academic-, financial-, and gender-related compliance issues; and serve as the public faces of their institutions' athletic programs by talking with media and fans. Athletic directors may also be called *directors of athletics, athletic directors of intercollegiate athletics,* and *athletic administrators.*

HISTORY

The National Collegiate Athletic Association (NCAA) was formed in 1905 to address violence in intercollegiate football. Around this time, the position of athletic director was formally created by college administrators who saw the need for experienced professionals to run their institutions' athletic programs.

After World War II, the NCAA began to regulate and monitor recruiting and financial aid issues. With rule changes and NCAA regulation, college athletics blossomed in the second half of the 20th century. Athletic directors played an important role in the growth of collegiate athletics during this time, but it was not until the First and Second National Conferences on Athletic Administration in Colleges and Universities in 1959 and 1962, respectively, that these professionals began to take the first steps toward creating a professional organization.

At the third such conference in 1965, the National Association of Collegiate Directors of Athletics (NACDA) was founded to serve the needs of athletic directors at junior and four-year colleges. The association boasts a membership of over 6,000 athletic directors and associate and assistant athletic directors at NCAA, National Association of Intercollegiate Athletics (NAIA), and National Junior College Athletic Association (NJCAA) colleges throughout the United States.

In 1979, the Council of Collegiate Women Athletic Administrators was created to enhance opportunities for women in intercollegiate athletics. To better represent its members, the Council was renamed the National Association of Collegiate Women Athletic Administrators (NACWAA) in 1992. The NACWAA has nearly 1,200 members.

THE JOB

Athletic directors plan and implement athletic programs at colleges and universities. Athletic directors at large Division I schools oversee large budgets, supervise staffs that range from dozens to hundreds of employees, and make many important decisions daily. They are helped by assistant and associate athletic directors who specialize in financial, media relations, compliance, and other issues. Athletic directors at large schools spend much of their time raising money and marketing their programs to the public. At small colleges, athletic directors work alone or with very small staffs. In addition to their main duties, they might drive athletes to games, coach sports teams, write press releases or marketing copy, and teach classes. The work of athletic directors can be divided into the following general areas: staff management/administration, financial issues, compliance, and public relations.

Staff management/administration. Athletic directors hire and supervise coaches and other department staff. They evaluate the performance of coaches and give them feedback. Athletic directors may have to fire coaches who fail to perform up to expectations.

Athletic directors have many administrative duties. They oversee coaches, athletic teams, and employees who assist with ticket sales, fund-raising, public relations, and other tasks. They make sure that stadiums, playing fields, and training, locker, and weight rooms are in good condition. Athletic directors meet with athletic directors from other schools and conference and association officials to coordinate athletic schedules and discuss rules and regulations. They meet with faculty representatives regarding academic issues relating to student athletes.

Financial issues. Athletic directors create and manage the athletic budgets at their institutions. When creating budgets, they make sure that each sport is allotted enough money to operate effectively. Athletic directors must be aware of their institutions' spending rules, as well as the regulations established by the NCAA, the NAIA, and the NJCAA. They plan and oversee ticket sales and certify income reports from these sales. Athletic directors negotiate radio and television broadcasting contracts and other commercial contracts and agreements that earn revenue for their institutions. This revenue is used for scholarships, team equipment, travel expenses, coaching and administrative staff salaries, the design and printing of schedules and marketing materials, and other expenses. Revenue also comes from fans (known as *boosters*), who make donations to the program. Athletic directors must be expert fund-raisers to make up for any budget shortfalls.

Compliance. One of the most critical tasks for athletic directors is navigating compliance issues relating to academic achievement, scholarships, gender issues, and other regulations established by their institutions; athletic conferences; the NCAA, NAIA, and NJCAA; and the federal government. They monitor the academic and graduation rates of student athletes and meet with student athletes, parents, and faculty to resolve problems. If an athletic director's institution participates in federal student financial aid programs, they must prepare an annual Equity in Athletics Disclosure Act Report to account for scholarships. The director must also ensure that the institution is compliant with Title IX regulations, which guarantee the equal participation of women in collegiate sports.

Public relations. Athletic directors must be highly skilled at public relations. They need to develop strong relationships with donors and booster organizations that help raise much-needed revenue for their departments. They also speak at high schools, fan fests, and sports awards dinners. They oversee staff that produces and disseminates public relations material about the athletic program.

Athletic directors meet with newspaper, radio, and television reporters almost daily. They answer a variety of questions from these media professionals. They might be asked about the job security of the women's basketball coach, a generous gift to the athletic department by a donor, or the construction of the school's new multipurpose sports arena. Athletic directors speak at news conferences, on sports talk shows, and at other media events.

Athletic directors employed at small schools may only work part time. They spend the rest of their time teaching classes, chairing the physical education department, or coaching sports. All athletic directors, whether employed by a tiny sports program or a major, well-known program, must have a vision for the future of their programs. They must be able to explain this vision to administration officials, the media, and fans.

REQUIREMENTS

High School

A well-rounded education is important for anyone interested in becoming an athletic director. In high school, take accounting, mathematics, business, social studies, and other college preparatory classes. Since communication skills are of utmost importance to athletic directors, be sure to take English and speech courses as well.

Postsecondary Training

A bachelor's degree in sports administration, physical education, or a related field is the minimum educational requirement to become an athletic director. You will need a graduate degree to be hired by the best programs.

Ohio University in Athens, Ohio, has the oldest program in the country in sports administration. Administered by the School of Recreation and Sports Sciences within Ohio University's College of Health and Human Services, the program requires 55 credit hours (five of which are completed during an internship) and leads to the master of sports administration degree. The curriculum focuses on business administration, journalism, communications, management, marketing, sports administration, and facility management. The required internship lasts from three months to a year, and internship opportunities are provided by more than 400 different organizations worldwide.

Other Requirements

To be successful in this career, you need to have a love and knowledge of sports. Since athletic directors must juggle many different tasks at once, you need to be organized and able to delegate tasks. Developing strong people skills will help you work effectively with people from all types of backgrounds. You must be dedicated to academic excellence and have a high degree of integrity, as well as have strong management and leadership skills. Athletic directors are under constant pressure to create winning, financially sound programs. For this reason, you must be emotionally steady, a good judge of coaching ability, and expert at business and financial management.

EXPLORING

Reading industry publications is a good way to learn more about this career. The NACDA publishes *Athletics Administration*, a bimonthly journal that focuses on issues in collegiate athletics administration. The journal also has a Q&A Forum, where leading athletic directors are interviewed about current issues in the field. To learn more, visit the NACDA's website, http://www.nacda.com. The NACWAA publishes the *NACWAA Newsletter*. Recent issues featured articles on writing top-flight resumes and developing leadership skills. Visit http://www.nacwaa.org to read a sample issue of the newsletter.

If your high school has a large sports program, it might employ an athletic director. If so, talk with this person about his or her career. Ask them about their primary and secondary job duties, the type of training they received to qualify for the job, how they were hired for this position, and how working as a high school athletic director compares to working at the college level. If your school doesn't employ an athletic director, ask your guidance counselor or physical education teacher to set up an informational interview with one at a nearby college.

EMPLOYERS

Nearly every college and university in the United States employs athletic directors. Opportunities exist at private and public institutions, community colleges, and universities both large and small. At a smaller college, a coach, not a traditional administrator, may serve as the athletic director. High schools with large sports programs may also employ athletic directors.

STARTING OUT

Professional publications such as *The Chronicle of Higher Education* (http://www.chronicle.com) and *NCAA News* (http://www.ncaa.org/employment.html) have job listings for athletic directors. The human resources departments in most colleges and universities maintain listings of job openings at the institution and often advertise the positions nationally. The College and University Professional Association for Human Resources also has job listings at its website, http://www.cupahr.org.

Landing a job as an athletic director can be difficult; dozens of applicants may apply for a single position. For this reason, it is very important that you gain experience in the field and develop good networking skills. Work as a coach, assistant athletic director, or physical education instructor, or in another related position to get experience. Take advantage of any networking opportunities (league meetings, trade shows, association membership) to get to know others working in the field. Some of the best job leads in the industry come by word of mouth. The NACDA also offers internships for aspiring athletic administrators.

ADVANCEMENT

Athletic directors advance by taking positions at larger schools or at institutions that have better known athletic programs. For example, an athletic director at a small Division II school might take a job at a larger, Division I institution. Or a director who is already at the top college level may take a position at a school that has a better-known athletic program. Some athletic directors become administrators in professional sports, commissioners of athletic conferences, or recreation administrators for cities or towns. Others choose to leave the profession entirely, working as deans or academic advisers at their universities.

EARNINGS

Salaries for college administrators vary widely among two-year and four-year colleges and among public and private institutions, but they are generally comparable to those of college faculty. According to the U.S. Department of Labor's *2001 National Occupational Employment and Wage Estimates,* the median salary for education administrators (which include athletic directors) was $61,700. The lowest paid 10 percent of administrators earned $33,640 or less per year, while the highest paid made $112,620 or more annually.

Most athletics directors receive benefits packages that include health insurance, paid vacation, and sick leave.

WORK ENVIRONMENT

Athletic directors work in a typical business office setting. Athletic directors at large schools have their own offices and large administrative staffs, while directors at small schools may have to share an office and do much of the work associated with this position themselves.

Athletic directors often work more than 40 hours a week, including evenings and weekends. They travel to professional conferences, to league meetings, and to other colleges for important games. They might be on the road an entire weekend for an important football game or a few weekdays for league or association meetings.

OUTLOOK

The U.S. Department of Labor predicts that overall employment for education administrators (which include athletic directors) will grow about as fast as the average through 2010. Athletic directors have little job security. They often lose their jobs if their athletic program fails to meet expectations. The total number of athletic directors employed by colleges and universities remains fairly steady. Some new opportunities may become available as colleges add athletic programs. Competition for these positions, however, will be stiff.

FOR MORE INFORMATION

For information on internships, educational opportunities, job listings, and the journal Athletics Administration, contact
National Association of Collegiate Directors of Athletics
PO Box 16428
Cleveland, OH 44116
Tel. 440-892-4000
http://www.nacda.com

For information on student membership and the NACWAA Newsletter, contact
National Association of Collegiate Women Athletic Administrators (NACWAA)
4701 Wrightsville Avenue
Oak Park D-1
Wilmington, NC 28403
Tel: 910-793-8244
http://www.nacwaa.org

For information on the master of sports administration degree, contact
Sports Administration/Facility Management Program
Ohio University
School of Recreation and Sport Sciences
E148 Grover Center

Athens, OH 45701-2979
Tel: 740-593-4666
Email: sportsad@ohiou.edu
http://www.cats.ohiou.edu/sportadmin

━━━━━━━━ INTERVIEW ━━━━━━━━

Valerie J. Cushman is the Athletic Director at Randolph-Macon Woman's College in Lynchburg, Virginia. She spoke to the editors of Careers in Focus: Coaches & Fitness Professionals *about her career.*

Q. Please describe your primary and secondary job duties.

A. Since 1997, I have served as the director of athletics, chair of physical education, and an assistant professor of physical education at Randolph-Macon Woman's College. I am responsible for implementing and maintaining programs and policies that support the philosophy of Randolph-Macon Woman's College, the Old Dominion Athletic Conference, and the National Collegiate Athletic Association. It is my responsibility to develop and implement all aspects of the intercollegiate athletics program and physical education department. My responsibilities include:

- coordination of daily operations of the intercollegiate athletic program
- creation and implementation of the physical education curriculum
- hiring, supervising, and evaluating coaches, faculty, and administrative personnel
- financial planning, budget preparation, and budget allocation
- teaching classes in the physical education curriculum
- serving as a representative at conference and affiliation meetings
- membership on college, conference, and association committees

Q. Where do you work? Do you travel for your job?

A. I work mostly indoors, but with a healthy dose of outdoor activity through home game management duties. I travel to national and regional conference and committee meetings, important away matches, and professional development opportunities.

Q. What was your college major? How did you train for this job?

A. I received a B.S. in physical education from SUNY-Cortland, an M.S. in physical education/sport management from East Stroudsburg University, and a Ph.D. in higher education from Syracuse University. In addition to my formal education, I received hands-on experience through work as a student employee in the athletics department at my undergraduate institution, as well as by taking advantage of internship and graduate assistantship opportunities.

Q. How did you get your first job in this field?

A. My first job was a college-level coaching/teaching position that I obtained after completing an internship at that institution (Vassar College).

Q. How can women learn more about this field?

A. For women interested in the field, the National Association of Collegiate Women Athletic Administrators is an outstanding support/educational group.

Q. What are the most important personal and professional qualities for athletic directors?

A. Personal qualities: You need to enjoy sports, have a lot of energy, be flexible, like to assist in the development of students, and have a sense of humor.

Professional qualities: You should have good interpersonal, organizational, and communication skills (both oral and written).

Q. What are some of the pros and cons of your job?

A. Pros
- something different every day
- autonomy
- good opportunity to make a difference in the life/development of a coach or student
- some, but not all, desk work
- challenging in a variety of ways
- plenty of measuring sticks of success

Cons
- long hours including nights and weekends
- can't control all factors (such as budget and wins and losses)

Q. What is the most important piece of advice that you have to offer college students as they graduate and look for jobs in this field?

A. Gain as much hands-on experience as you can and network in the field through participation in professional development opportunities.

Q. What is the future employment outlook for athletic directors?

A. Good, especially for women!

College Sports Coaches

OVERVIEW

College sports coaches teach individuals or members of a team the skills associated with a particular sport. A coach prepares his or her team for competition and gives instruction from a vantage point near the playing area during competition. There are over 90,000 elementary, secondary, postsecondary, and professional sports coaches employed in the United States.

HISTORY

The first intercollegiate sports contest in the United States was held between Harvard University and Yale University in 1852. Harvard defeated Yale in a crew (rowing) contest that was watched by hundreds, and possibly thousands, of spectators. In 1856, Harvard University, Brown University, Yale University, and Trinity College formed the College Rowing Association.

During the 1860s and 1870s, baseball, football, and track and field became popular intercollegiate sports. According to Andrew Zimbalist's *Unpaid Professionals: Commercialism and Conflict in Big-Time Sports* (Princeton University Press, 2001), college football games were attracting tens of thousands of fans and earning colleges and universities significant revenues by the 1880s.

The National Collegiate Athletic Association (NCAA) was formed in 1905 to reform intercollegiate football, where the lack of protective equipment and the dangerous flying wedge formation had caused 330 player deaths between 1890 and 1905. After World War II, the

NCAA began to regulate and monitor recruiting and financial aid issues. With rule changes and NCAA regulation, college athletics blossomed in the second half of the 20th century.

Today, college athletics is big business in the United States, and top-performing college sports coaches and players—especially in men's Division I basketball and football programs—earn their universities millions of dollars in broadcasting and marketing revenue.

In addition to such high-profile sports as basketball and football, college coaches teach male and female athletes baseball, cross country, fencing, field hockey, golf, gymnastics, ice hockey, lacrosse, rowing, skiing, soccer, softball, swimming/diving, tennis, track, volleyball, water polo, and wrestling.

THE JOB

Regardless of the sport they coach—whether it is men's Division I-A college basketball, women's softball at a tiny Division III school, or wrestling at a junior college—college sports coaches are teachers. They must be able to teach their athletes the rules, techniques, and strategies for their respective sports. If they are unable to convey this knowledge, their athletes won't be able to improve their performance and win games.

To teach athletes, coaches plan and implement training and practice sessions. During these sessions, they teach players proper rules, stances, and movements of a game. Coaches use lectures and demonstrations to show their players the proper way to compete in the sport. They point out mistakes and deficiencies and help players to improve their overall performance. Coaches oversee practices and workouts to help athletes develop fundamentals and condition their bodies for the rigors of competition.

In addition to physical preparation, college sports coaches must prepare their players mentally for competition. They give pep talks before, during, and after games to help build players' confidence. During a losing streak, a coach might give his or her team a pep talk to encourage team members to remain confident in their abilities, or may speak to an individual player who has lost confidence in his or her play. Conversely, a coach might talk with his or her team during a long winning streak to ensure that the players do not become overconfident. Some college coaches have a very emotional style that often inspires their players to top performance. This style can backfire if a coach becomes too emotional or even confrontational when dealing with his or her players. A good coach realizes that yelling or even berating players for mistakes or poor play tends to create negative results.

College sports coaches also help their players develop good sportsmanship, ethics, and academic excellence. They teach their players how to act on and off the playing field. They might institute a dress code or a code of conduct for their players to encourage discipline and appropriate behavior. Coaches may act as mentors to players who are experiencing personal problems. They also work to ensure that each of their players meets NCAA academic requirements. Players who fail to meet these requirements cannot play until they improve their grades.

To prepare for competition, coaches meet with their assistant coaches to formulate and develop game plans. They explain and demonstrate their game plans to players during practice. For example, a basketball coach may teach his or her players a new defensive strategy that aims to stop the opposing team's top scorer. A baseball coach may educate his or her hitters about a weakness discovered by watching game film of the opposing team's starting pitcher. A golf coach may discuss the challenges of the course for the next match. Coaches also choose a starting lineup and determine substitution patterns for the remaining players. They must make sure that each player knows what his or her role will be during the game.

During competition, coaches discuss strategy with assistant coaches, yell out plays or encouragement to their players, prepare players who are about to enter the game, and call timeouts when necessary. They analyze the play of their team and the opposing team and change game plans if necessary during timeouts or other breaks in action. For example, a college basketball coach may notice that the opposing team's players are tiring and take advantage of this by instructing his or her players to play a more aggressive defense.

Coaches must know the mental and physical abilities of their players and use this knowledge to make split-second decisions during competition. They must know who is their most tenacious defender, who is their best scorer, and who performs best under intense pressure. This knowledge, combined with their coaching acumen and the performance of players, can make the difference between losing and winning.

Coaches of individual-player sports, such as track or tennis, usually do most of their coaching in practice before the competition. Athletes must then apply these coaching lessons to competition. During competition, coaches encourage players, offer tips to improve their performance, and take notes on their performance and technique for use in future practices.

Coaches need to be willing to learn new coaching techniques. Many attend clinics or seminars to learn more about their individual sports or how to teach players more effectively. Many coaches are members of professional organizations that deal exclusively with their individual sports.

Coaches should be strong communicators, since they are often interviewed by print, radio, and television reporters. They also make appearances at fundraisers, fan fests, and other events.

Coaches also have administrative duties. During the off season, college coaches actively recruit new players to join their teams. They travel across the country and even the world to scout promising high school players who might be a good fit for their team. They meet with promising players and their parents and offer scholarships to try to convince these players to attend their college and play for their team.

REQUIREMENTS

High School
To prepare for college, take human physiology, psychology, biology, health, and exercise classes. Courses in English and speech will help you to develop your communication skills. Playing and coaching sports is one of the best ways to learn more about this career while you are in high school. If you can't play or coach sports, volunteer to work as a team statistician, equipment manager, or sports reporter on your school's newspaper. These jobs will allow you to observe coaches at work.

Postsecondary Training
Though there is no standard educational path for aspiring coaches, most college coaches have bachelor's degrees. Some college coaches were student athletes in college, while others attended college and received their degrees without playing a sport. Most college coaches begin their careers at small colleges where teaching is part of their job duties. To become a college teacher, you will need to earn at least a bachelor's degree in education or another subject area.

Other Requirements
To be a successful college coach, you need to be extremely knowledgeable about your sport, including its rules and strategies. You need to be an effective communicator in order to be able to teach your

A college football coach gives a player last-minute advice before he heads back out on the field. (Jim Whitmer Photography)

players the fundamentals of your sport, impart game strategies, and encourage team play.

Coaches must be steady, disciplined leaders who are able to patiently instruct players as they practice plays and techniques over and over. They must keep in mind that all athletes learn and improve at different rates. Coaches should be optimistic and have strong motivational skills. They should maintain the same professional demeanor whether they are winning or losing games.

Coaches must be able to work well under pressure as they guide their teams through games and tournaments that carry great personal stakes for everyone involved.

EXPLORING

If you are interested in a career in coaching, get involved with playing and coaching sports as early as possible. Play as many high school sports as you can. Volunteer to assist coaches of Little League baseball, Pop Warner football, or other youth leagues. Work as a counselor or coach at a summer sports camp. Ask your school counselor to set up an interview with a local coach. These activities will help you discover if coaching is something that you enjoy.

You might also consider subscribing to publications such as *Coaching Digest* (baseball, http://www.abca.org), *Extra Point* (football, http://www.afca.com), *Basketball Sense* (http://www.basketballsense.com), and *Soccer Journal* (http://www.nscaa.com). These magazines are geared toward coaches, players, and fans who are interested in sports coaching. Visit the websites of these organizations to read sample issues and articles.

EMPLOYERS

Most of the over 4,000 two- and four-year colleges and universities in the United States have sports programs that employ sports coaches. Besides working for colleges, coaches are employed by high schools, professional sports teams, individual athletes, youth leagues, summer camps, and recreation centers. After finishing their coaching careers, some college coaches pursue opportunities in broadcasting or work as motivational speakers.

STARTING OUT

Aspiring college coaches often begin their careers by working as high school coaches, youth league coaches, or recreation center coaches. One of the best ways to get coaching experience at the college level is to work as a *graduate assistant coach*. Graduate assistant coaches are recent graduates who are interested in becoming coaches. They receive a stipend and gain valuable coaching experience assisting head coaches.

ADVANCEMENT

A typical advancement path for a successful coach might be from high school coach, to assistant college coach, to head coach at a junior college, to head coach at a small Division I program. Successful Division I college coaches can advance to become assistant and head coaches for professional sports teams. Some coaches never become head coaches but have fulfilling careers as assistant coaches at the amateur and professional levels.

EARNINGS

The U.S. Department of Labor reports that the median earnings for sports coaches were $29,030 in 2001. The lowest paid 10 percent earned less than $13,410, while the highest paid 10 percent earned more than $62,560. Sports coaches who worked at colleges and universities earned a median annual salary of $32,880 in 2000.

College head football coaches earn an average of approximately $75,000 annually, although top coaches can earn as much as $2 million per year.

In 2000–01, head coaches in men's Division I basketball earned average salaries of $115,586, according to the Women's Basketball Coaches Association. Head coaches in women's Division I basketball averaged $86,199 during that same time span. Some top coaches in men's Division I basketball earn salaries of $1 million or more, according to sportsillustrated.com. For example, Tubby Smith, men's basketball coach at the University of Kentucky, earns approximately $2.42 million annually, while Roy Williams, men's basketball coach at the University of North Carolina, earns nearly $1.1 million annually.

Many popular coaches augment their salaries with income from personal appearances and endorsements.

WORK ENVIRONMENT

College sports coaches work indoors in climate-controlled conditions and outdoors in conditions that range from comfortable to hot, humid, cold, rainy, and snowy. In outdoor stadiums, weather conditions may affect a team's performance.

College teams compete throughout the United States and Canada. They travel by bus, train, or plane to competitions. Players and coaches stay in hotels while on the road.

Many college coaches work part time, with teaching or other activities filling the remainder of their time. Coaches in high-profile college sports such as football and basketball may work year-round. During the sports season, coaches may work up to 16 hours a day, five or six days each week. Games often occur on nights and weekends.

There is very little job security in college coaching. Athletic directors expect their coaches to consistently win, especially in such financially lucrative sports as football and basketball. Coaches are often fired if their teams do not perform up to expectations.

OUTLOOK

Although the U.S. Department of Labor predicts that the occupation of sports coaching will grow about as fast as the average, the number of college coaching opportunities is not expected to increase. Some colleges have cut less-popular sports programs, which has reduced the number of coaching positions. Openings will be available as coaches retire or are terminated. However, coaches have little job security unless they can consistently produce winning teams.

FOR MORE INFORMATION

For certification information, trade journals, job listings, and a list of graduate schools, visit the AAHPERD website.

> **American Alliance for Health, Physical Education, Recreation and Dance (AAHPERD)**
> 1900 Association Drive
> Reston, VA 20191-1598
> Tel: 800-213-7193
> http://www.aahperd.org

For information on membership and baseball coaching education, coaching Web links, and job listings, visit the ABCA website.

> **American Baseball Coaches Association (ABCA)**
> 108 South University Avenue, Suite 3
> Mount Pleasant, MI 48858-2327
> Tel: 989-775-3300
> Email: abca@abca.org
> http://www.abca.org

For information on football coaching careers, contact

> **American Football Coaches Association**
> 100 Legends Lane
> Waco, TX 76706
> Tel: 254-754-9900
> Email: info@afca.com
> http://www.afca.com

For informational on hockey coaching, contact

> **American Hockey Coaches Association**
> 7 Concord Street
> Gloucester, MA 01930
> http://www.ahcahockey.com

For information on careers in sports and physical education, contact

> **National Association for Sport and Physical Education**
> 1900 Association Drive
> Reston, VA 20191-1598

Tel: 800-213-7193
Email: naspe@aahperd.org
http://www.aahperd.org/naspe

For information on basketball coaching, contact
National Association of Basketball Coaches
9300 West 110th Street, Suite 640
Overland Park, KS 66210
Tel: 913-469-1001
http://nabc.ocsn.com

For information on college athletics, contact the following associations:
National Association of Intercollegiate Athletics
23500 West 105th Street
Olathe, KS 66051
Tel: 913-791-0044
http://www.naia.org

National Collegiate Athletic Association
PO Box 6222
Indianapolis, IN 46206-6222
Tel: 317-917-6222
http://ncaa.com

For information on the coaching of soccer, contact
National Soccer Coaches Association of America
6700 Squibb Road, Suite 215
Mission, KS 66202
Tel: 800-458-0678
http://www.nscaa.com

For information on women's basketball coaching, contact
Women's Basketball Coaches Association
4646 Lawrenceville Highway
Lilburn, GA 30047-3620
Tel: 770-279-8027
Email: wbca@wbca.org
http://www.wbca.org

Diet and Fitness Writers

QUICK FACTS

School Subjects
English
Health
Physical education

Personal Skills
Communication/ideas
Helping/teaching

Work Environment
Primarily indoors
Primarily one location

Minimum Education Level
Bachelor's degree

Salary Range
$20,570 to $42,450 to
$83,180+

Certification or Licensing
None available

Outlook
Faster than the average

DOT
131

GOE
01.01.02

NOC
5121

O*NET-SOC
27-3043.00

OVERVIEW

Diet and fitness writers express, edit, promote, and interpret ideas and facts about nutrition and exercise in written form for books, magazines, websites, trade journals, newspapers, technical studies and reports, and company newsletters.

These writers may report on their own experiences, or they may write about the diet or sports activities of others. Some diet and fitness writers create articles or full books on new dieting methods or exercise forms to persuade the general public to adopt the dieting or fitness trend.

HISTORY

Dieting and fitness may be buzzwords today, but they haven't always been on everyone's mind. The word "diet" actually refers to the food that one eats regularly, not an eating plan focused on restriction. This is why some people are said to have healthy diets, while many others follow poor diets (think fast food, convenience choices, and sugar- and fat-laden treats).

According to diet author Dr. Beth Gruber, one of the first individuals to put a diet into written form was an Englishman named William Banting. In 1850, Banting could hardly walk down the stairs or tie his own shoes because of his weight. In other words, he was obese (though this term had yet to be coined). After trying starvation, diuretics, and extreme exercise with no success, he met Dr. William Harvey, who recommended that Banting eliminate all sugar and starches from his diet.

34

This finally brought success, and Banting lost 50 pounds at a safe rate. More importantly, he wrote about his experience, and his pamphlet titled *Letter On Corpulence Addressed to the Public* was read by people in countries around the world. Banting's work became the first written record of a diet that is still popular: the low-carbohydrate diet.

The need and desire to be fit has long been part of the human existence, from primitive man's needing to be quick and strong to hunt for food, to the first modern Olympic athletes in 1896 wanting to be quick and strong to win competitions.

In the United States, colonial life was tough enough that simple daily living required a good amount of fitness. According to Lance C. Dalleck and Len Kravitz, Ph.D., authors of *The History of Fitness,* early leaders such as Benjamin Franklin recommended a daily dose of exercise, including running, swimming, and even resistance training. President Thomas Jefferson also promoted the benefits of exercise, though possibly to extremes, recommending no less than two hours a day of physical activity.

Starting with the industrial revolution and continuing on to modern times, many jobs that once required physical effort are now done in part by machines and other forms of technology. As a result, people have become more sedentary, which has increased the need to find forms of exercise outside of physical labor.

One fitness pioneer was Jack LaLanne. In the 1950s, he hosted a successful television program that set the stage for other fitness personalities, such as Jane Fonda and Richard Simmons. LaLanne recommended a program of aerobic movement, either on a floor or in the water, and resistance training using machines with pulleys. He is even credited with inventing the (appropriately named) "jumping jack."

A more recent fitness pioneer is Dr. Ken H. Cooper, who, according to Dalleck and Kravitz, is recognized as the "father of the modern fitness movement." Cooper emphasizes using fitness not as a treatment course for disease, but as a method of disease prevention. LaLanne and Cooper have spurred many others to write about and promote their own recipes for fitness.

THE JOB

Diet and fitness writers work in the field of communications. Specifically, they deal with the written word, whether it is destined for the printed page, broadcast, or a computer screen. The nature of their work is as varied as the materials they produce. They may write health and fitness articles for books, magazines, and journals. They also contribute to scientific research and technical reports. Many writers promote a popular diet or fitness fad, such as the Atkins or Zone diets or the various forms of yoga. They may write advertisement copy or contribute to health and fitness segments for radio and television broadcasts.

Many successful diet and fitness writers have extensive educational or work experience related to their subject matter. However, those with specialized degrees and certifications must be able to communicate clearly with their intended audience. For example, a registered dietitian with an extensive background in biology and chemistry who writes for a general publication must be able to break down highly technical information on food composition into terms the average reader can understand and use.

Diet and fitness writers can be employed either as in-house staff or as freelancers. Pay varies according to experience and position, but freelancers must provide their own office space and equipment, such as computers and fax machines. Freelancers also are responsible for keeping tax records, sending out invoices, negotiating contracts, and providing their own health insurance.

REQUIREMENTS

High School
While in high school, build a broad educational foundation by taking courses in English, literature, health, science, computer science, and typing. An ability to type and a familiarity with computers are extremely important if you want to pursue a career in writing.

Postsecondary Training
Competition for writing jobs in the diet and fitness arena is very strong. A college education may not be required, but it helps to establish your skills as a writer. If you want to be hired full time as a diet or fitness writer, employers may prefer that you have a background in nutrition or sports fitness as well as course work in English or journalism. Some highly technical journals or scientific research publications require their writers to have a master's degree.

In addition to formal course work, most employers look for practical writing experience. Experience with high school and college newspapers, yearbooks, and literary magazines will make you a better candidate. In addition, experience with a small community newspaper, radio station, or local television station is also valuable. Many book publishers, magazines, newspapers, and radio and television stations have summer internship programs that provide valuable training if you want to learn about the publishing and broadcasting businesses. Interns do many simple tasks, such as running errands and answering phones, but some may be asked to perform research, conduct interviews, or even write some minor pieces. During these internships, express your interest in writing about health or fitness. That way, if such an assignment comes along, you may be the first to be asked to help out.

Certification and Licensing
Many diet and fitness writers also work as personal trainers, dietitians, nutritionists, or in other related careers. Many of these positions require additional education and certification to advise clients. For example, the American Council on Exercise and the American Fitness Professionals and Associates offer various types of certification, depending on your work interests. Individuals may choose to obtain certification as a trainer, nutrition consultant, exercise specialist, or pre/post-natal exercise instructor.

Other Requirements
To be a diet or fitness writer, you should be creative and able to express ideas clearly, have broad and specialized knowledge pertaining to your field of interest, be skilled in research techniques, and be computer literate. Other assets include curiosity, persistence, initiative, resourcefulness, and an accurate memory. For some jobs—on a health and fitness magazine staff, for example, where the activity is hectic and deadlines are short—the ability to concentrate and produce under pressure is essential.

EXPLORING

As a high school or college student, you can test your interest in and aptitude for the writing field by serving as a reporter or writer on school newspapers, yearbooks, and literary magazines. You should also explore the field of fitness and nutrition by participating in sports and taking part in health clinics or workshops.

Small community newspapers, magazines, and newsletters often welcome contributions from outside sources, although they may not have the resources to pay for submissions. Jobs in bookstores, magazine shops, and even newsstands will offer you a chance to become familiar with various publications, including those covering health, dieting, fitness, and sports.

You can also obtain information on writing careers by visiting local newspapers, publishers, or radio and television stations and interviewing some of the writers who work there. Career conferences and other guidance programs frequently include authors of all types from local or national organizations.

EMPLOYERS

Nearly one-fourth of all salaried writers work for newspapers, magazines, and book publishers, according to the *Occupational Outlook Handbook*. Health and fitness writers are also employed by advertising agencies and public relations firms, in radio and television broadcasting, and by journals and newsletters published by business and nonprofit organizations, such as the American Dietetic Association and the American Council on Exercise. Other employers include government agencies and websites. However, most diet and fitness writers are self-employed, working as freelancers for various magazines, book publishers, and websites that focus on health and sports.

STARTING OUT

A fair amount of experience is required to gain a full-time position as a diet and fitness writer. Most writers start out in entry-level positions. These jobs may be listed with college placement offices, or they may be obtained by applying directly to the employment departments of the individual publishers or broadcasting companies. Graduates who previously served internships often have the advantage of knowing someone who can give them a personal recommendation. Want ads in newspapers and trade journals are another source for jobs. Because of the competition for positions, however, few vacancies are listed with public or private employment agencies.

In most cases, employers will want to see your resume as well as samples of your published writing. These samples are often assembled in an organized portfolio or scrapbook. Bylined or signed articles are more credible (and, as a result, more useful) than stories whose source is not identified.

Beginning positions as a junior staff writer usually involve library research, preparation of rough drafts for part or all of a piece, cataloging, and other related writing tasks. These are generally carried on under the supervision of a more experienced writer or editor.

ADVANCEMENT

Diet and fitness writers may work full time in other fields and write on health or fitness topics in their free time. Once a writer is published, he or she can build a portfolio, gain a reputation as a writer, and possibly move into writing full time. Freelance or self-employed writers advance through increased exposure and established reputations.

Other diet or fitness writers find their first jobs as editorial or production assistants. Advancement may be more rapid in small companies, where beginners learn by doing a little bit of everything and may be given specialized writing tasks immediately. In large publishing houses or firms, duties are usually more compartmentalized. Assistants in entry-level positions are assigned such tasks as research, fact checking, and copywriting; it generally takes much longer to advance to full-scale writing duties.

Promotion into positions of higher responsibility may come with the assignment of more important or specialized articles and stories to write, or it may be the result of moving to another employer. Mobility among employees in this field is common. An assistant in one publishing house may switch to a higher level position in another. Or a writer may switch to a related job, such as personal trainer or dietitian, as a type of advancement.

EARNINGS

In 2001, median annual earnings for all salaried writers and authors were $42,450 a year, according to the Bureau of Labor Statistics. The lowest paid 10 percent earned less than $20,570, while the highest paid 10 percent earned $83,180 or more. In book publishing, some specialties pay better than others. Technical writers earned a median salary of $49,370 in 2001.

In addition to their salaries, many writers earn additional income from freelance work. Part-time freelancers may earn from $5,000 to $15,000 a year. Freelance earnings vary widely. Full-time established freelance writers may earn up to $75,000 a year.

WORK ENVIRONMENT

Working conditions vary for writers. Although full-time writers typically work 35–40 hours a week, many writers work overtime. A health or fitness publication that is published frequently has more deadlines closer together, creating greater pressures to meet them.

The work is especially hectic at newspapers and broadcasting companies, which operate seven days a week. These specialized writers often work nights and weekends to meet deadlines or to cover a last-minute story.

Most writers work independently, but they often must cooperate with artists, photographers, rewriters, and editors who may have widely differing ideas of how the materials should be prepared and presented.

Physical surroundings range from comfortable private offices to noisy, crowded newsrooms filled with other workers typing on their computers and talking on the telephone. Some writers must confine their research to the library or telephone interviews, but others may travel to other cities or countries or to local sites, such as restaurants, sports arenas, health centers, or other offices.

Freelance writers generally work from their own homes. As a result, they need a personal computer, printer, fax machine, copier, and possibly Internet access.

The work can be arduous, but most writers are seldom bored. The most difficult element is the continual pressure of deadlines. People who are the most content as writers enjoy and work well with deadline pressure.

OUTLOOK

The employment of all writers, including those specializing in diet and fitness topics, is expected to increase at a rate faster than the average for all occupations over the next several years, according to the U.S. Department of Labor. The demand for writers by newspapers, periodicals, book publishers, and nonprofit organizations is expected to increase. The growth of online publishing will also demand many talented writers; those with computer skills will have an advantage as a result.

The major book and magazine publishers, broadcasting companies, and the federal government account for the concentration of writers in large cities such as New York, Chicago, Los Angeles, Boston, Philadelphia, San Francisco, and Washington, D.C. Opportunities with small newspapers, corporations, and professional, technical, and trade publications can be found throughout the country.

People entering this field should realize that the competition for jobs is extremely keen. Beginners, especially, may have difficulty finding employment. Of the thousands who graduate each year with degrees in English, journalism, communications, and the liberal arts intending to establish a career as a writer, many turn to other occupations when they find that applicants far outnumber the job openings available. College students would do well to keep this in mind and prepare for a related alternate career in areas such as nutrition or physical education in the event they are unable to immediately obtain a position as a diet or fitness writer.

FOR MORE INFORMATION

For general health and fitness topics and to learn about fitness certifications, contact
American Council on Exercise
4851 Paramount Drive
San Diego, CA 92123
Tel: 800-825-3636
http://www.acefitness.org

The ADA is the single best source of information about careers in dietetics. Its website is an excellent resource that provides detailed information and links to other organizations and resources.
American Dietetic Association (ADA)
120 South Riverside Plaza, Suite 2000
Chicago, IL 60606-6995
Tel: 800-877-1600
http://www.eatright.org

For information on home study and various fitness certifications, contact
American Fitness Professionals and Associates
PO Box 214
Ship Bottom, NJ 08008
Tel: 609-978-7583
Email: afpa@afpafitness.com
http://www.afpafitness.com

For educational and career information, contact
American Society for Nutritional Sciences
9650 Rockville Pike, Suite 4500
Bethesda, MD 20814
Tel: 301-530-7050
http://www.asns.org

For general educational information on all areas of journalism, including newspapers, magazines, television, and radio, contact

Association for Education in Journalism and Mass
  Communication
234 Outlet Pointe Boulevard
Columbia, SC 29210-5667
Tel: 803-798-0271
http://www.aejmc.org

INTERVIEW

Sky Taylor is the host and author of a nutrition and fitness website called Diet Bites (http://www.dietbites.com). She is also a nutritionist and has been working one-on-one with clients for many years. She spoke with the editors of Careers in Focus: Coaches & Fitness Professionals *about her work as a diet and fitness author and her educational background.*

Q. Please briefly describe your primary and secondary job duties.

A. My primary focus is creating unique and sometimes off-the-wall material that will build an interested audience. Dieting, losing weight, getting fit—it can be quite tricky because there's no magical product to achieve success! The key is providing the audience (our readers) with motivational articles and information that they can trust, and articles that will help them achieve their weight loss and fitness goals.

My secondary job duty is to maintain the Diet Bites website. Some of these tasks include purchasing graphics, making graphics, learning software programs that build Web pages, interacting with our hosting service, and answering emails from individuals seeking to lose weight.

Q. Do you travel for your job?

A. Although travel is not necessary for my job, it's very useful because it provides insight to other cultures throughout the country. Foods are often prepared differently in different regions of the country; in fact, even the foods available in one geographic area may be entirely different from another area. These things are not only interesting to know, but are a great help when writing Web content.

Q. How did you train for this job? What did you study in college?

A. Like most writers, I began writing at a very early age. Yes, from the beginning the writing was on the wall; actually, on my mother's wall. (Literally, gold on white paint—my hand took on a life of its own.) Needless to say, my mother wasn't very happy, but things improved with age, as they generally do. As I grew older, I always had a story to tell or share, and so I would put those on paper.

A good writer is an avid reader, so even now, I read as much as I can on a variety of subjects. My college courses included nutrition and business management.

Q. Did your educational training prepare you for this career, or would you pursue another major if you could start over today?

A. As for the writing side of me, I wouldn't have done much differently. However, most anyone can be a nutritionist, so I would definitely have steered my career towards becoming a dietitian.

Q. How can someone learn more about writing? What tips would you give to writers trying to break into this field?

A. The local library is always a wonderful place to begin your writing journey. Many cities have writing clubs where writers can interact with one another. When you begin writing, be willing to "give a little free ink." Many times, webmasters are searching for well-written, inexpensive content. So you might try volunteering to write a commentary-type article.

In addition, as a writer beginning a professional career, it's good to know that there are great writers, there are good writers, and there are some really bad writers. But even a really bad writer will stand a far better chance of publication by targeting the appropriate market.

Try to submit to the markets that parallel closest what you have written. It's smart to read a publication from the market in which you are submitting. This will help you iron out any potential rough spots in your completed piece in the event your work is accepted. There is nothing more painstaking than to have the perfect article or script and be asked to rewrite what may be a perfectly wonderful piece because it doesn't fit the mold of the market. So research those markets! Inform yourself of the direction, philosophy, requirements, and distribution of the targeted publisher.

Q. What are the most important personal and professional qualities for writers?

A. Personal: Writers who have the ability to see both sides of a story or situation are usually the forerunners in their field. Some people see what they want to see, but a good writer sees what is really there.

Professional: Courtesy, tact, diplomacy, and compassion are important qualities. Be prepared to accept rejections as challenges, and use what you learn to grow.

Q. What are some of the pros and cons of your career?

A. Oddly enough, the pros and cons of this job are the same! Cons: There are periods when I'm really busy. Around Christmas and the New Year, I have to write many of the articles well in advance. The New Year, with all its resolutions, brings the best opportunity in getting individuals motivated to either lose unwanted weight or to get healthier.

Pros: Because articles are sometimes written well in advance, it gives me the opportunity to keep a watchful eye on events and health trends that can be incorporated into the final article.

Q. What advice would you give to people who are interested in entering this field?

A. Determine not only the marketability of your work, but also how "sellable" it will be a few months or years down the road. Just because a topic was hot one year ago doesn't mean it's still hot now. People tend to drift towards change because it keeps things exciting. Is your finished work riding a crest or is it a dying trend? Is it unique? Independent, yet in bounds with the market you are submitting to? Is it immensely rewarding? Will it tap new reading experiences?

The bottom line is generally always money. Consider the time constraints and cost of production of your work. Is it doable? With a little research and ingenuity, you can send your finished work in the right direction, and in the process, ensure a greater measure of success. Most importantly, never give up! Keep submitting for the writer within you!

As to the weight-loss coaching aspect, you'll want to keep in mind that individuals may be dancing the diet jig one day, and then running towards a pantry stocked with cream-filled sponge cakes the next. Therefore, try to establish, as well as maintain, a professional rapport with the individuals you are coaching.

This was one of my downfalls when I began weight-loss coaching. A good example is the time I helped a wonderful woman lose 65 pounds. Then she went away for a summer vacation filled with fun (and fatty) foods. We kept in touch via email, and I kept hearing that all was fine. However, when she returned, she had definitely gotten into more than just a little cheese, because she'd packed back on the 65 pounds plus another 12. I think I cried for two hours, at least. So, don't allow yourself to become a personal buddy to your clients. Remember, you're the coach! When an individual does fall off the weight-loss wagon, help them back up and motivate them to try again.

Remember, writers are unique artists and are born, rather than self-made. Follow your dreams and ALWAYS look back, because therein you'll sometimes find that hidden gem of a story!

Dietitians and Nutritionists

QUICK FACTS

School Subjects
Chemistry
Family and consumer science
Health

Personal Skills
Helping/teaching
Technical/scientific

Work Environment
Primarily indoors
Primarily one location

Minimum Education Level
Bachelor's degree

Salary Range
$25,230 to $40,410 to
$56,870 +

Certification or Licensing
Required in some states

Outlook
About as fast as the average

DOT
077

GOE
N/A

NOC
3132

O*NET-SOC
29-1031.00

OVERVIEW

Registered dietitians (RDs) are professionals who have met certain educational requirements and passed a national certification exam. For the purposes of this article, the terms "dietitian" and "registered dietitian" will be used interchangeably. RDs provide people with foods and dietary advice that will improve or maintain their health. They may be self-employed or work for institutions, such as hospitals, schools, restaurants, and nursing homes—any place where food is served or nutritional counseling is required. Hospital dietitians, for example, may ensure that the food served in the cafeteria is nourishing or create special diets for patients with particular nutritional problems and needs.

Regulation of those using the professional title *nutritionist* varies by state. For example, in some states a person without any specialized training may be able to call himself or herself a nutritionist and offer dietary advice. For the purposes of this article, however, the term "nutritionist" refers to *certified clinical nutritionists* (CCNs) who have received specialized training and passed a certification exam. CCNs usually work in private practice and are concerned with the biochemical aspects of nutrition.

Today there are approximately 49,000 dietitians and nutritionists working in the United States.

HISTORY

Nutrition has always been an important concern to people throughout the world, and the use of food as medicine has been recognized throughout recorded history. In India, the form of medicine known as Ayurveda, which tailors diets to individuals to cure or to maintain health, has been practiced for almost as 5,000 years. Traditional Chinese medicine, which is approximately as old as Ayurveda, makes use of many dietary recommendations and proscriptions. Both forms of medicine are still widely used in their countries of origin, and both have spread to other parts of the world.

In ancient Greece, philosophers and healers noted the connection between diet and health, and ultimately it was the Greek practice of careful observation and research that gave rise to the scientific method on which modern Western nutrition is based. It should be understood, however, that observation and research were also important parts of virtually all other medical traditions.

A major breakthrough in nutrition occurred in the 18th century, when the French chemist Antoine-Laurent Lavoisier began to study the way the body uses food energy, or calories. He also examined the relationship between heat production and the use of energy, and his work has caused him to be known as the "father of nutrition."

By the early 20th century, vitamins had been studied, and the relationship between diets and certain illnesses came to be understood. By 1940, most vitamins and minerals had been discovered and studied, and the field of nutrition had made tremendous strides. Since that time, advances in technology have enabled scientists to learn far more about nutrition than was possible earlier. At present, much is known, but much remains to be learned. It often happens that one study contradicts another regarding the benefits or dangers of certain foods.

THE JOB

Registered dietitians have a broad-based knowledge of foods, dietetics, and food service. They have at least a bachelor's degree in food science or related field from a school accredited by the Commission on Accreditation for Dietetics Education (CADE), have completed a CADE-accredited internship, and have passed a registration exam. The term "nutritionist" can refer to a variety of people because regulations covering the use of this title vary from state to state. In some states, anyone—even those with little or no specialized education or credentials—can set up shop as a nutritionist. CCNs are specialists who have completed a certain amount of postgraduate education that focuses on the biochemical and physiological aspects of nutrition science. In all other respects, they have the same core educational and internship backgrounds as RDs.

There are many practice areas within the rapidly growing and changing field of nutrition. One reason for this growth is that the public has become more aware of the importance of nutrition in recent years, and this development has opened up new areas for dietitians and nutritionists. The list of specialties that follows is by no means exhaustive.

Clinical dietitians are in charge of planning and supervising the preparation of diets designed for specific patients, and they work for such institutions as hospitals and retirement homes. In many cases, their patients cannot eat certain foods for medical reasons, such as diabetes or liver failure, and the dietitians must see that these patients receive nourishing meals. Clinical dietitians work closely with doctors, who advise them regarding the patients' health and the foods that the patients cannot eat. It is often part of a clinical dietitian's job to educate patients about nutritional principles.

Community dietitians usually work for clinics, government health programs, social service agencies, or similar organizations. They counsel individuals or advise the members of certain groups—such as the elderly, families, and pregnant women—regarding nutritional problems, proper eating, and sensible grocery shopping.

Although most dietitians do some kind of teaching in the course of their work, *teaching dietitians* specialize in education. They usually work for hospitals, and they may teach full time or part time. Sometimes teaching dietitians also perform other tasks, such as running a food-service operation, especially in small colleges. In larger institutions, however, those tasks are generally performed by different people. In some cases, teaching dietitians also perform research.

There are many kinds of *consultant dietitians,* who work for such organizations as schools, restaurants, grocery store chains, manufacturers of food-service equipment, pharmaceutical companies, and private companies of various kinds. Some of these organizations have home economics departments that need the services of dietitians. Some consultants spend much of their time advising individuals rather than organizations. One lucrative area for consultants is working with athletes and sports teams, helping to maximize athletes' performance and extend the length of their careers.

Administrative dietitians, also known as *management dietitians,* combine management skills with people skills to organize and run

Diet and Nutrition Glossary

A (vitamin): nutrient found in animal products such as egg yolk, milk, and fish liver oils that helps to prevent visual defects

aerobic exercise: physical activity, such as running, that requires the use of oxygen

anaerobic exercise: physical exertion that causes an oxygen debt

anorexia: eating disorder categorized by starvation or extremely low calorie intake that results in dangerously low, and sometimes fatal, body weight

B (vitamin): group of water-soluble vitamins found in yeast, eggs, liver, and some vegetables that aids in metabolic functions

basal metabolism: lowest rate of calorie burn that results from breathing, sleeping, and otherwise remaining at rest

binge eating: eating large quantities of food out of an emotional compulsion, not out of hunger; often followed by purging, or vomiting

C (vitamin): nutrient found in citrus fruits and leafy vegetables that prevents scurvy, a disease which affects the teeth and gums and can cause excessive bleeding

caffeine: natural stimulant found in food and drinks such as chocolate, coffee, and tea

carbohydrate: compound, composed of sugars, used by the body for energy

cholesterol: a lipid, or fat; can be affected by LDLs and HDLs; LDLs (low-density lipoproteins), found in fatty fish such as salmon, is a healthy substance that carries cholesterol to help build and repair cells; HDLs (high-density lipoproteins), found in saturated fat in foods such as in baked goods, are unhealthy and contribute to the blocking of arteries

D (vitamin): fat-soluble vitamin found in milk, fish oil, and egg yolk that promotes bone and tooth growth and repair

daily value (DV): recommended intake amounts (of sodium, carbohydrates, and protein, for example) that have been developed by the Food and Drug Administration to be used on food labels

diabetes: disease that prevents the production of insulin to break down and use food for energy; Type 1 diabetics do not produce insulin at all and must take insulin injections; Type 2 diabetics produce insulin but have an excess amount of fat cells that cannot absorb and use insulin

diuretics: substances, such as alcohol, that encourage the elimination of water from the body through urination; can cause mild dehydration

Continues

Continued

E (vitamin): nutrient found in leaves and seed germ oils that prevents infertility, muscle deterioration, and vascular disease

energy: body's capacity to do work

fat: substance that is solid at room temperature, but liquid at hot temperature; also can be used to describe all lipids

glucose: blood sugar

hypertension: high blood pressure

hypotension: low blood pressure

insulin: hormone produced by the pancreas that help the body carry and use blood sugar

lactose: carbohydrate that is found in milk and other dairy products; some individuals are lactose intolerant, meaning they lack the sufficient amount of the enzyme needed to break down and digest this carbohydrate

lipids: family of compounds that includes fats and oils

metabolism: chemical changes within cells that provides energy for the body

morbid obesity: weighing 100 to 149 percent above the recommended weight bracket based on gender and height

nutrients: substances obtained from food used for energy and the growth and repair of cells

obesity: having excessively high levels of body fat in relation to lean tissue

Recommended Daily Allowance (RDA): recommended amounts of energy and nutrients to meet the needs of average healthy individuals

saturated fat: fat, generally from animal sources, that is fully loaded with hydrogen; because of this chemical makeup, it is hard for the body to digest

unsaturated fat: fat, from plant and fish sources, that is missing hydrogen from its chemical makeup and is easier for the body to break down

vegan: vegetarian who eats only plant-based foods

vegetarian: individual who abstains from eating some or all animal-based foods

Source: Physicians Weight Loss Centers (http://www.pwlc.com)

large-scale food operations. They may work for food-service companies, oversee the cafeterias of large corporations, be employed by prisons, or work at long-term-care facilities—basically they work for any organization that provides food services to a large number of people. In addition to planning menus, dietitians are responsible for such things as creating budgets, drawing up work policies, and enforcing institutional and government regulations that relate to safety and sanitation.

Research dietitians typically work for government organizations, universities, hospitals, pharmaceutical companies, and manufacturers, and they may specialize in any of a vast number of research subjects. They often work on improving existing food products or to finding alternatives to foods that are unhealthy when eaten in substantial portions.

Certified clinical nutritionists typically work in private practice for themselves, as part of a group of health care professionals, or for a doctor or doctors in private practice. CCNs are specialists who have completed at least some postgraduate training in nutrition science. They work with clients to correct imbalances in the clients' biochemistry and improve their physiological function. Through lab tests, consultations with doctors, and discussions with the clients themselves, CCNs review the clients' overall health and lifestyle and determine what nutrients the clients have too little or too much of. They then come up with plans to enable their clients to get the correct nutrition to get their bodies back into balance. Their clients may range from people who are slightly ill, for example, those who feel run down all the time but don't know why, to people with serious diseases, such as heart disease or cancer. No matter what problem brings a client to a CCN, though, the CCN's goal is to correct that client's biochemistry in order to help that person feel better.

REQUIREMENTS

High School

If you want to be a dietitian or a nutritionist, you should take as many courses as possible in health, biology, chemistry, family and consumer science, and mathematics. If you are not sufficiently prepared in high school, you are likely to struggle with such college courses as mathematics and biochemistry. Communication skills are also important, since dietitians and nutritionists must interact effectively with clients, employers, and colleagues. Even researchers who spend most of their time in the lab must cooperate with colleagues and write clear, accurate reports on the results of their work. For this reason, dietitians and nutritionists must be well versed in spoken and written English. Psychology, which generally is taught in college nutrition programs, is an important aspect of the work of many dietitians and nutritionists.

Postsecondary Training
There are a couple different educational routes you can choose from to become a dietitian. The first is to complete a bachelor's or master's level CADE-accredited coordinated program that combines classroom work with 900 hours of supervised internship experience. Currently there are 52 programs of this type. Once you have graduated, you are eligible to take the registration exam. Another option is to get at least your bachelor's degree from a CADE-accredited program that provides only classroom instruction. After receiving your degree you then need to get 900 hours of hands-on experience through a CADE-accredited practice program or internship. Currently there are 263 accredited internship programs, which take six to 24 months to complete (depending on whether you are on a full- or part-time schedule). Once you have completed both of these steps, you are eligible to take the registration exam. The American Dietetic Association (ADA) notes that there is no list of courses all would-be dietitians should take. However, the ADA does provide the *Directory of Dietetic Programs* of selected programs that meet CADE standards. In addition, the ADA website (http://www.eatright.org/cade) also provides a listing of these schools. Those who enter this field typically get degrees in food and nutrition science, dietetics, food service, or other related areas. Course work may include classes in economics, business management, culinary arts, biochemistry, physiology, and food science. If you want to teach, do research, or work in public health, you should get a bachelor's degree and one or more advanced degrees.

Nutritionists complete the same type of undergraduate education as dietitians, including fulfilling the 900 hours of a supervised internship. They must also complete at minimum a certain number of courses at the master's degree level to be eligible to sit for the clinical nutritionist certification exam. Many actually complete a master's or Ph.D. in nutrition science.

Certification or Licensing
Currently 45 states have laws regulating the practice of dietitians and nutritionists through licensure, certification, or registration. Of these states, 30 require licensure, 14 require certification, and one requires registration.

The registered dietitian (RD) credential is awarded by the Commission on Dietetic Registration of the ADA. To receive this designation, dietitians must have completed CADE-approved education and training and pass the registration exam. To maintain their standing, registered dietitians must also complete continuing education on a regular basis. Some specialty certifications, such as board certified specialist in pediatric nutrition (CSP), are also available through the ADA.

The CCN credential is awarded by the Clinical Nutrition Certification Board of the International and American Associations of Clinical Nutritionists. To receive this designation, nutritionists must have completed a bachelor's degree (which includes certain classes in the sciences and nutrition), done postgraduate studies in clinical nutrition, finished an internship, and passed the written examination. Recertification is required every five years.

Other Requirements

Because there are so many technical requirements in the field of nutrition, dietitians and nutritionists must be detail oriented and able to think analytically. Math and science are a major part of both training and work. Dietitians and nutritionists must be comfortable making decisions and acting on them. Even those who do not work as consultants have to be disciplined and decisive.

For most dietitians, flexibility is crucial. Karen Petty, R.D., an administrator who began her career as a clinical dietitian, says about working in institutional food service: "You will never be able to please everyone, because everyone has different tastes in food. You learn to be able to take criticism and go on to try to please the majority."

People who want to become administrators must have people skills. On that subject, Petty says: "When I'm asked what is the hardest part of my job, I never hesitate to say it's personnel management." For administrators, the ability to communicate clearly and effectively is particularly important.

EXPLORING

You can start exploring this type of work right in your own kitchen. Learn healthy ways to cook and bake. Plan and prepare meals for your family; do your own grocery shopping and learn to pick out the best produce, meats, fish, and other ingredients. And, in addition to taking family and consumer science classes at school, take cooking classes offered by other organizations in your community. Supermarkets, for example, frequently offer classes on topics such as how to prepare low cholesterol meals. Another option is to contact dietitians and nutritionists and ask them about their work. The school cafeteria, the local hospital, or a nursing home are all places to look for those who would be willing to have an informational interview with you. And, of course, one of the best ways to learn about nutrition is to get a job in a food-related business such as a restaurant or a hospital cafeteria. In such a setting, you will be able to observe and interact with dietitians as they work.

EMPLOYERS

Many kinds of government and private organizations hire dietitians, and the kinds of available opportunities continue to increase. There are opportunities in hospitals, schools of all levels, community health programs, day care centers, correctional facilities, health clubs, weight-management clinics, health management organizations, nursing homes, government organizations, food-service companies, food equipment manufacturers, sports teams, pharmaceutical companies, and grocery store chains, to name a few. Among the large organizations that need dietitians are the armed forces, which have to feed their personnel as well and as inexpensively as possible. In addition, dietitians and nutritionists can work in private practice, running their own consulting businesses or working in a group practice.

STARTING OUT

Because dietitians and nutritionists are extensively trained and have some practical experience before they look for their first job, they tend to know the type of organization they want to work for. Most colleges and universities provide placement services, and people often find work through connections they make at school or in practice programs. For this reason, it is wise to make as many professional connections as possible.

Some parts of the country have more dietitians and nutritionists than others, and beginning dietitians should consider taking positions out of their areas in order to get started in the business. Jobs can be found via trade journals, national and state conventions, websites, classified ads, and specialized employment agencies. Although it is possible to call organizations to learn about job opportunities, the most effective way to find work is through personal contacts.

ADVANCEMENT

There are various ways to advance in the business. One of the best is further education. RDs with only a bachelor's degree may wish to obtain an advanced degree, which will enable them to apply for research, teaching, or public health positions that are not otherwise open to them. For example, a dietitian interested in working in community dietetics may get an advanced degree in public health; someone wanting to move into management may get a master's in business administration. RDs can also advance by getting further education that leads to specialty certification, such as the CCN or the CSP. Often advancement depends upon the goals of the individual, as he or she decides where to go with this career.

In the field of nutrition, as in most others, seniority, reliability, expertise, and experience count. An experienced clinical dietitian might ultimately become an administrative dietitian, for example, and a research dietitian might take charge of a research department.

EARNINGS

Salaries vary by practice area, years of experience, educational level, and location. In general, administrative, self-employed, and business dietitians earn more than their clinical and community counterparts.

According to the Bureau of Labor Statistics, the median annual salary for dietitians and nutritionists was $40,410 in 2001. The lowest paid 10 percent earned less than $25,230; the highest paid 10 percent earned more than $56,870 a year.

The ADA reports findings from its membership indicate that of dietitians employed for five years or less, 61 percent had yearly earnings in the $25,000–$35,000 range and 26 percent of this group earned between $35,000 and $45,000. The ADA also found that RDs in business, private practice, and consulting earned more than $50,000 per year.

In addition to salary, most employers also offer benefits packages including health and life insurance, paid vacations and holidays, and a pension or profit-sharing plan.

WORK ENVIRONMENT

Nutritionists usually work in medical office settings that are clean, well lit, and organized. Dietitians generally work in offices or kitchens. Such environments are usually clean and well lit, although some kitchens may be hot and stifling. Some dietitians and nutritionists sit much of the time, while others spend all day on their feet. Most work 40-hour weeks, but some—especially dietitians who work for hospitals and restaurants—are required to work on weekends and at odd hours. Part-time positions are also common.

Some hospitals offer dietitians room, board, and laundry services for a nominal fee, but this arrangement is becoming less common. In the past, many college dietitians lived in apartments provided by the school, but this arrangement is also becoming a thing of the past, except where dietitians run food-service operations in residence halls.

Benefits such as health insurance, sick pay, vacations, and 401-K plans are as prevalent in the field of nutrition as they are in other fields. Naturally, dietitians who run their own businesses must make their own arrangements in these areas.

OUTLOOK

According to the U.S. Department of Labor, employment of dietitians and nutritionists will grow about as fast as the average for all occupations over the next several years. One contributor to continued growth is the public's increasing awareness of the importance of nutrition. Another contributing factor is the fact that the population is aging rapidly, which will bring about an increased need for nutritional counseling and planning in nursing homes, home health care agencies, community health programs, and prisons. Hospital dietitians may experience growth somewhat slower than others in the industry. This is because inpatient treatment is expected to decline, while outpatient treatment will increase. Many hospitals are expected to hire contractors to handle food-service operations.

FOR MORE INFORMATION

The ADA is the single best source of information about careers in dietetics. Its website is an excellent resource that provides detailed information and links to other organizations and resources.
American Dietetic Association (ADA)
120 South Riverside Plaza, Suite 2000
Chicago, IL 60606-6995
Tel: 312-899-0040
http://www.eatright.org

The goal of the ASNS is to improve people's quality of life through the nutritional sciences. It is a good source of educational and career information.
American Society for Nutritional Sciences (ASNS)
9650 Rockville Pike, Suite 4500
Bethesda, MD 20814
Tel: 301-530-7050
http://www.asns.org

For information on dietitian certification, contact
Commission on Dietetic Registration
120 South Riverside Plaza, Suite 2000
Chicago, IL 60606-6995
Tel: 312-899-0040, ext. 5500
Email: cdr@eatright.org
http://www.cdrnet.org

For more information on becoming a certified clinical nutritionist,
contact
International and American Associations of Clinical Nutritionists
16775 Addison Road, Suite 100
Addison, TX 75001
Tel: 972-407-9089
http://www.iaacn.org

Fitness Directors

QUICK FACTS

School Subjects
Health
Physical education

Personal Skills
Communication/ideas
Helping/teaching

Work Environment
Primarily indoors
Primarily multiple locations

Minimum Education Level
Some postsecondary training

Salary Range
$25,170 to $49,810 to
$95,300+

Certification or Licensing
Voluntary

Outlook
Faster than the average

DOT
N/A

GOE
N/A

NOC
0513

O*NET-SOC
39-1021.00

OVERVIEW

Fitness directors organize and schedule exercise classes and programs for health clubs, resorts, cruise lines, corporations, and other institutions. They work with other fitness professionals, such as personal trainers, nutritionists, and health care personnel, to deliver the best services for the individuals who use the fitness facility. Fitness directors must balance the needs of their staff with the needs of the paying customers. To do this, directors listen to suggestions from staff and clients regarding program changes or additions, instructor criticisms, and any other comments to make sure the fitness facility runs smoothly and paying customers are happy.

HISTORY

Ask most people what they'd like to change about their lifestyle, and many of them will answer, "to exercise more and get in better shape." The desire to be fit is not a recent development, but there are many more options available today than ever in the past.

The fitness industry has seen many changes. Not so long ago, men worked out by pumping iron in their basements, while women were more prone to working out in front of a television to exercise videos and programs. Now, you can go to a health club for an aerobics class and facial all in one day. Exercise is no longer simply something you have to do alone in your basement or in a sweaty, smelly gym. Today, people have options to get in shape. You can work out while on vacation, during your lunch hour in your office building, between classes at school, or even, for the young, at your local day care center. Fitness has become more accessible and easier to incorporate into our busy work and social lives.

In addition, expanded fitness programming is appealing to a larger audience than before. Programming used to be dominated by floor aerobics. Now, you can take a class in urban dance, spinning (cycling), or body pump (weight lifting). All of these options are possible because of the hard work and organizational skills of fitness directors.

THE JOB

Fitness directors are a crucial part of sports and health facilities. They coordinate the schedules of exercise instructors and personal trainers. They also make sure that their institution offers a wide variety of options to keep customers happy. For example, a fitness director who works at a nursing home must plan and direct classes that appeal to an older population. This director ensures that instructors have experience working with the elderly and then arranges for a class that is low impact or held in a swimming pool. Exercise classes can be held even while clients remain seated.

On a cruise ship, fitness directors must cater to a wide variety of clients. There may be children on board who would enjoy exercising through games (such as Duck, Duck, Goose) while their parents might enjoy a step aerobics class to help counter all the food eaten that day at the buffet. Creating and maintaining this balancing act is a large part of the fitness director's job.

In addition to planning class schedules, directors oversee the overall operation of the fitness facility, making sure equipment and rooms are clean, exercise machines are operating correctly, and the temperature of rooms is comfortable.

Directors must also be observant and make improvements to the programming schedule. For example, perhaps a water aerobics class has not been well attended and is taking up unnecessary lanes in the pool. The facility's fitness director, after talking to lap swimmers that exercise at that time, might decide to eliminate or move the water aerobics class to another time slot, or simply reserve fewer lanes for the class. These are the types of adjustments that directors make on a monthly, if not weekly, basis to keep customers happy.

Because many clients may feel uncomfortable making suggestions or complaints about a class directly to an instructor, fitness directors also serve as a sounding board. Perhaps participants in an aerobics class are having a hard time hearing the instructor over the music.

In this case, a class member can bring the complaint to the attention of the fitness director, who in turn might provide the instructor with a cordless microphone to use during class. Fitness directors keep the peace in health and sports facilities and, as a result, help to keep the facilities in business.

REQUIREMENTS

High School
If you're interested in working in a health and fitness facility, take science and physical education classes and get involved in sports activities. It's also important to take home economics classes, which include lessons in diet and nutrition. Business courses can help you prepare for the management aspect of the job.

Postsecondary Training
Fitness directors should have a background in exercise science to be able to serve their clients and understand the needs of their fitness facility. Associate and bachelor's degree programs in health education, exercise and sports science, fitness program management, and athletic training are offered in colleges all over the country. Typical classes include nutrition education and consulting, anatomy and physiology, business management, biochemistry, and kinesiology. Because the job of fitness director is a higher management position, most employers will require a bachelor's degree in a sports fitness field and many years of experience in the fitness industry.

Certification or Licensing
Certification in fitness or exercise science is highly recommended (if not required) to work in a management-level position at a fitness facility. Because there are many kinds of certification available, you should choose a certifying board that offers scientifically based exams and requires continuing education credits. The American Council on Exercise (ACE) and the American Fitness Professionals and Associates (AFPA) are just two of the many organizations with certification programs. Some employers also require that their fitness staff members be certified in cardiopulmonary resuscitation (CPR).

Other Requirements
Fitness directors not only need to know about the industry in which they work, but they also have to be comfortable with managing staff. This requires organization, flexibility, and strong communication skills. A friendly disposition and good people skills are also essential.

EXPLORING

To explore this career, be sure to get fit yourself! If your school offers exercise classes or some other after-school fitness program, sign up and note what you like and dislike about instructor methods or the environment. If there is an affordable gym or health club in your community, take a tour and even a sample class or two. Some clubs offer guest passes for a small fee so prospective members can try out a facility before committing to a membership.

While at the facility, talk to an instructor, manager, or trainer about his or her job and work environment and how to best break into the industry. This way, you can learn about what goes into developing, running, and maintaining a fitness program.

You may even be able to obtain a part-time job at your school or community recreation and fitness center. This would be a great experience and would give you the chance to see if you enjoy working in fitness.

EMPLOYERS

Fitness directors work in health clubs, gyms, corporate fitness centers, day care centers, nursing homes, hospitals, rehabilitation centers, resorts, and for cruise lines. Health and sports centers are located in urban, suburban, and rural areas all over the country.

STARTING OUT

Most fitness directors start out in another career within the sports, health care, or fitness industries. They may start out as personal trainers, aerobics instructors, or physical therapists and move into managerial positions that involve more responsibility and earning potential. Those looking to break into a fitness career should be sure they have the appropriate knowledge and certifications before applying for positions. Health and fitness centers within gyms, resorts, corporate buildings, and cruise ships may advertise open positions in the newspaper or online at their websites. Professional associations, such as the Medical Fitness Association and the Aerobics and Fitness Association of America, have job boards that post openings in centers all over the country.

ADVANCEMENT

Because the job of fitness trainer is a higher level management position, advancement is limited to moving to the same position within a larger fitness institution or becoming an owner of a fitness facility.

EARNINGS

Because many fitness trainers start out in other positions, earnings can vary. Many individuals who eventually become directors major in exercise science. According to the American Society of Exercise Physiology, the salaries for those who have earned degrees in exercise science are as follows: bachelor's, $18,000–$25,000; master's, $22,000–$32,000; and doctorate, $30,000–$60,000.

Once in a management position, fitness directors can earn much more, but their salaries still vary considerably depending on their experience and the size and location of their facility. Administrative services managers (the category under which the U.S. Department of Labor classifies fitness directors) earned median annual salaries of $49,810 in 2001. The lowest paid 10 percent earned less than $25,170, and the highest paid 10 percent earned $95,300 or more per year.

WORK ENVIRONMENT

With the pressure of balancing the needs of both clients and staff members, the job of fitness director can be demanding. However, the majority of directors work in comfortable workplaces. Most facilities maintain a cool temperature, are clean and well lit, and have well-cared-for equipment. Directors who work part time usually have to pay for their own benefits.

OUTLOOK

Opportunities within the fitness industry should grow more quickly than the average over the next several years. In general, people are much more knowledgeable about exercise and nutrition. Businesses and medical professionals are promoting exercise as beneficial for both good health and increased work productivity. As the baby boomers grow older, they will increasingly rely on gyms, health clubs, and other fitness facilities to stay in shape. Knowledge of special weight training, stretching exercises, and diets for seniors will also drive older individuals to fitness institutions in the years to come.

FOR MORE INFORMATION

For a listing of jobs and certification information, contact
   Aerobics and Fitness Association of America
   15250 Ventura Boulevard, Suite 200
   Sherman Oaks, CA 91403-3297
   Email: contactAFAA@afaa.com
   http://www.afaa.com

For general health and fitness topics, and to learn about certification,
contact
   American Council on Exercise
   4851 Paramount Drive
   San Diego, CA 92123
   Tel: 800-825-3636
   http://www.acefitness.org

For information on certification, contact
   American Fitness Professionals and Associates
   PO Box 214
   Ship Bottom, NJ 08008
   Tel: 609-978-7583
   Email: afpa@afpafitness.com
   http://www.afpafitness.com

For a listing of jobs in the fitness industry, contact
   Medical Fitness Association
   PO Box 73103
   Richmond, VA 23235-8026
   Tel: 804-327-0330
   http://www.medicalfitness.org

Health Club Owners
and Managers

QUICK FACTS

School Subjects
Business
English

Personal Skills
Communication/ideas
Leadership/management

Work Environment
Primarily indoors
Primarily one location

Minimum Education Level
Bachelor's degree

Salary Range
$25,170 to $49,810 to
$95,300+

Certification or Licensing
Recommended

Outlook
Faster than the average

DOT
339

GOE
11.11.02

NOC
0651

O*NET-SOC
39-1021.00

OVERVIEW

Health club owners and managers are responsible for the overall success of a fitness facility. Club owners buy, sell, and lease facilities, oversee top management, and play a role in the hiring and firing of staff. Club managers handle the daily operations of the club, such as hiring, training, and scheduling staff members, planning fitness programming, checking exercise equipment, and ensuring the safety and cleanliness of the club.

HISTORY

Medical professionals have long toted exercise as beneficial (if not necessary) to maintain health. In addition to a nutritional diet, daily exercise helps to maintain weight, aids circulation, and promotes lung and heart health. Many exercise by running, walking, biking, or skating in the great outdoors. However, for many people who live in harsh climates during much of the year, this is not always possible. There needs to be another option for those in Arizona in the middle of summer or those in Minnesota in the dead of winter. The introduction and rapid expansion of health clubs across the country fit this need.

According to an article by Phil Kaplan in *Muscle & Fitness* magazine, experts predict clubs will attract approximately 50 million members and will create 50,000 full-time and 150,000 part-time positions in the industry by 2010.

THE JOB

In general terms, health club managers, like other facility managers, coordinate the events that occur in the club with the services and people who make those events possible. This involves planning exercise programs, hiring trainers and class instructors, supervising facility redesign and construction, and overseeing the custodial staff who keep the club clean and safe. Depending on the size of the health club, managers may have different job titles and specialized duties, such as fitness directors (see the separate article on this career) or membership managers.

Health club owners are concerned with much more than the internal workings of the club. Owners need to have enough money to keep the club running, and managers are responsible for maintaining those finances. This may require months, if not years, of research and long-term financial planning. Another crucial issue club owners must consider is how their club compares to others in the area. Does their club offer enough fitness options? Are the club's hours flexible for members with varying schedules? Is the cost of membership fair and competitive with other clubs? To determine these answers, owners may visit other health clubs to investigate their design, organization, and the types of classes offered.

Many health club owners expand their business beyond one location. To choose a new site, owners must analyze their finances and ensure that there is enough local support for a new club. Owners also must be aware of the area's zoning laws or other federal, state, and local regulations concerning the construction of new buildings.

In general, health club owners and managers spend most of their time in the office or somewhere within the health club itself, supervising the day-to-day management of the facility. Club owners determine the organizational structure of the facility and set personnel staffing requirements. As staffing needs arise, the club manager addresses them with the owner, who then sets the education, experience, and performance standards for each position. Depending on the size of the facility and the nature of managers' assigned responsibilities, hiring may be conducted by a separate personnel director or by the club's general manager.

REQUIREMENTS

High School

High school courses that will give you a general background for work in health club ownership or management include business, health, mathematics, physical education, and computer science.

Speech and writing classes will help you hone your communication skills. Managing a school club or other organization will give you an introduction to overseeing budgets and the work of others.

Postsecondary Training

A bachelor's degree is generally required to own or manage a heath club. Many owners and managers first work in lesser positions within the fitness industry to establish backgrounds in health or exercise science. The competition for jobs and increased complexity of owning and managing a facility (keeping the club in business and profitable) requires a strong background in business and finance. Many owners and managers hold a master's degree in business administration or sports facility management.

Certification or Licensing

Put simply, health clubs can bring owners a large amount of revenue, and these owners aren't willing to trust the management of such lucrative venues to individuals who are not qualified to run them. Certification is one way a health club owner can ensure that certain industry standards in club management are met. The International Facility Management Association (IFMA), probably the industry leader in certification, offers the designation of certified facility manager (CFM). The International Association of Assembly Managers also offers the certification designation of certified facilities executive (CFE). For contact information for these associations, see the end of this article.

Other Requirements

Most club owners require that higher level managers have a minimum of five years of experience in the field or industry. This may include experience in other manager positions or in related fitness careers. Many managers end up in their management positions after first working as one of the club's staff members, such as an aerobics instructor or personal trainer.

In addition to experience, both owners and managers need to be strong communicators to work well with staff and relate well to the club's members. They need to be able to state their ideas, information, and goals clearly and concisely, regardless of their audience.

Health club owners, in particular, need to possess excellent strategic, budgetary, and operational planning skills to keep the club in business and to ensure profits. The owner's decisions affect all operations within the health club, so the owner needs to be capable of making the right choices and have the ability to juggle many different tasks.

Exercise Myths

MYTH: To see maximum results, you need to push yourself to the limits.

TRUTH: Pushing yourself to the point of exhaustion, or worse, pain, will only invite injury. It's okay to have an occasional tough workout, but use sense when exercising. You should be able to get up and be active again the next day!

MYTH: Women who weight train will become big and bulky.

TRUTH: Unlike men, women don't have enough natural testosterone to become bulky from lifting. Weight training, when done correctly, will tone muscles and actually help women look leaner, not bigger.

MYTH: To tighten a flabby stomach, all you need to do are sit-ups.

TRUTH: Spot reducing is not possible. The only way to lose the flab is through a healthy diet and exercise—for all your body parts.

MYTH: Some diet supplements can block fats from being absorbed by the body.

TRUTH: Many of these supplements are not only scams (and a waste of money), but may also be dangerous to your health. The only way to lose weight is through healthy eating and activity.

MYTH: To be effective, working out requires a lot of time.

TRUTH: While you won't see results immediately, just 30 minutes a day will improve your overall health and fitness. Roughly an hour a day is recommended if you are looking to lose weight.

Source: American Council on Exercise

EXPLORING

To be able to understand and meet the requirements of a health club career, you should be familiar with sports and fitness. Become involved in a sports team while in high school, as either a team member or a manager. Any and all experience helps, whether you're a star player, an equipment manager, or the team's statistician. You can also work with a local Booster Club to sponsor events that promote sports and fitness within your school district. These activities demonstrate your interest and devotion to sports and fitness and may help in the future by providing you with an edge when searching for a job.

Be sure to visit a health club, whether it is a small gym in your school or a large club in your neighborhood. While visiting, take some mental notes about the size and roles of the club's staff. Do you notice a manager on duty? How many pieces of exercise equipment are available? Is the club clean? If possible, ask a staff member about his or her job and how to get started in the industry. If you visit a local health club, ask if you can work out as a guest for a small fee. This will allow you to experience a club firsthand.

College students interested in sports facility management may be able to locate valuable internships through contacts they have developed from part-time jobs, but the placement centers in undergraduate or graduate programs in business administration and facility management are also good places to find information on internships.

EMPLOYERS

There are over 14,000 commercial health clubs currently in operation. Fitness facilities may be chain operations or local establishments, or they may be owned by a larger corporation that offers the facility solely for the benefit of its employees.

STARTING OUT

Because of their growing popularity, health clubs offer more part- and full-time positions than ever before. To find an employer near you, check for classified ads in local newspapers or online. You could also look up "health clubs" in a phone book and call or visit those in your area to ask about job opportunities.

Graduates of programs in sports administration and sports facility management usually find jobs through past internships, from personal contacts they developed in the field, or from job listings in their graduate programs' placement departments.

Many health club managers start out in other jobs. They may move into a management position after working in another fitness career. For example, an aerobics instructor who desires more management duties may become the club's fitness director. Other club managers are hired after first working in business. For example, a public relations professional who is dedicated to working out may choose to leave his or her industry to work in health and fitness instead.

The job of health club owner is not a starting position. Most owners start out in other fitness industry positions, gaining the experience and financial know-how that are necessary for running a business.

ADVANCEMENT

Experience and certification are the best ways for someone to advance in a fitness career. Years of successful, on-the-job experience count for a great deal in this industry. Health club owners look for managers who have demonstrated the ability to run a club smoothly. Certification is another way in which success can be gauged. Since certification goes hand-in-hand with experience, it is assumed that those individuals who are certified are the best in their field.

Apart from experience and certification, a willingness and eagerness to learn and branch into new areas is another important factor affecting advancement. Those who are willing to embrace new technology and are open to new ideas and methods for improving the operation of their clubs will likely advance in their careers.

Health club managers who have strong business sense and financial backing may advance further by deciding to own their own clubs.

EARNINGS

Earnings for health club owners and managers depend on their experience and education, as well as the size of the facility. Administrative services managers (the category under which the U.S. Department of Labor classifies sports and fitness facility managers) earned median annual salaries of $49,810 in 2001. The lowest paid 10 percent earned less than $25,170, and the highest paid 10 percent earned $95,300 or more per year. Club managers who are certified earn higher salaries than those who are not certified. The International Facility Management Association reports that members who held the CFM designation earn an average of $8,000 more than their noncertified counterparts.

WORK ENVIRONMENT

Health club owners and managers work in clean, comfortable surroundings. However, their jobs can be stressful and often require the ability to juggle many tasks at once. Managers and owners must constantly deal with the challenge of balancing the needs of staff members with the needs of the club's members—needs that may, at times, be at odds with each other.

Depending on the size of the club, the workload of owners and managers often requires that they work more than a standard eight-hour day. Managers are generally compensated for overtime by additional pay or time off. For owners, extra hours go unpaid; overtime simply comes with the territory of running a business.

OUTLOOK

The U.S. Department of Labor predicts faster than average growth for the fitness industry. Because a growing number of people realize the importance of daily exercise for their general health and well being, health clubs should continue to enjoy growth and popularity in the coming years. As the number of health clubs increases, so too will the demand for qualified individuals able to run them.

FOR MORE INFORMATION

For general health and fitness information, contact
   American Council on Exercise
   4851 Paramount Drive
   San Diego, CA 92123
   Tel: 800-825-3636
   http://www.acefitness.org

IDEA conducts surveys, provides continuing education, and publishes a number of books and magazines relevant to the fitness industry. For more information, contact
   IDEA, Inc.
   6190 Cornerstone Court East, #204
   San Diego, CA 92121-3773
   Tel: 800-999-4332, ext. 7
   Email: nonmemberquestions@ideafit.com
   http://www.ideafit.com

For certification information, job listings, student chapters, and internships, contact
   International Association of Assembly Managers
   635 Fritz Drive, Suite 100
   Coppell, TX 75019-4442
   Tel: 972-906-7441
   http://www.iaam.org

For information on certification, contact
International Facility Management Association
1 East Greenway Plaza, Suite 1100
Houston, TX 77046-0194
Tel: 713-623-4362
Email: ifmahq@ifma.org
http://www.ifma.org

To find the health club, fitness center, or gym nearest you, check out the following website:
HealthClubDirectory.com
http://www.healthclubdirectory.com

INTERVIEW

Fran Beckmann is a group exercise director at a health club in Chicago. She spoke with the editors of Careers in Focus: Coaches & Fitness Professionals *about her educational background and work experience.*

Q. What are your main duties at the health club?

A. • Planning, organizing, scheduling, and staffing all of the club's group exercise programs. This includes more than 150 classes per week that our club offers to members in a variety of formats, such as Pilates, yoga, spinning, boxing, body pump, water aerobics, hip-hop dance, ballet, children's classes, and many other strength and cardio exercise classes.

• Managing (which involves recruiting, interviewing, hiring, training, evaluating, and paying) a staff of more than 90 group exercise instructors and professionals who teach the classes we offer.

• Assembling and organizing a printed brochure distributed to members three times a year that details all the club's services and activities. This involves coordinating information from all the departments (personal training, massage, climbing, kid's club, and membership.)

• Handing communication and follow-up from member questions, concerns, complaints, and general feedback regarding any classes and instructors.

• Ordering, maintaining, and tracking all of the club's equipment needed for classes, including aerobic steps, weights, and microphone systems.

- Teaching six classes per week on the club's group exercise schedule, including two spinning, two step aerobics, and two Fittrek (outdoor walking) classes. This keeps me connected to the members, and I share the same responsibilities as my staff of instructors.
- Assisting and supporting other managers in daily operations.
- Planning and scheduling any certifications or instructor trainings that are hosted at the club. These are usually held on weekends and require much planning in advance.
- Attending fitness conventions and seminars to stay on top of what is going on in the fitness industry.

Q. Where do you work? Do you travel for your job?

A. I work mostly indoors, although I teach an outdoor walking class (Fittrek) twice a week, in the rain, snow—any temperature. I used to travel for my job on weekends as a Spinning presenter and trainer. I taught other instructors how to teach spinning in over 26 states around the country. This was challenging, but I learned a lot about how other clubs set up their programs.

Q. How did you train for this job?

A. I became certified through the Aerobics and Fitness Association of America as a group exercise instructor and later as a personal trainer. I started teaching in San Francisco twice a week to develop my skills and become a good instructor. Before I took this, I taught 16 classes per week at eight different health clubs in the Chicago area. This gave me the experience working with people of various ages, skill levels, and attitudes.

In college, I studied business management; however, once I entered the fitness industry, I never planned to work in business.

Q. Would you have pursued another major?

A. I probably would have chosen an exercise science degree for this field.

Q. Where did you get your first job?

A. My first job was with a small health club called Island Athletics in Fremont, California. It was located 20 miles from my house, I had to take public transportation to get there, and I received $5 for each class that I taught.

Q. What kinds of resources are available to someone looking to enter this field?

A. Many directors start out as fitness instructors, and there are plenty of certifications you can earn to provide you with the knowledge needed to teach. However, obtaining certification doesn't ensure you'll succeed. It is hard to get hired without experience. For this reason, I suggest finding a role model instructor who is willing to work with you. It takes a lot of practice.

Q. What are some personal and professional qualities needed for people in your career?

A. To organize and schedule exercise classes that members will enjoy, you need to stay fresh, inspired, and creative. Also, as a fitness professional, you need to take care of your own body, which includes eating well and sleeping enough. It's easy to burn out or take on too much and get injured in this profession.

Q. What are the pros and cons of your job?

A. Pros: The health club is also a fun environment and, as a result, working there doesn't always feel like "work."

Cons: Because you are constantly dealing with club members or staff, you should always act energetic and motivated—even if you're not. Sometimes you have to turn off what's going on within you to be able to work with a big smile.

Q. What advice can you share with those hoping to get into the fitness industry?

A. If you actually love what you do and you're good at it, money will eventually come. It may take a little longer than you thought, but stay with it!

Lifeguards and Swimming Instructors

OVERVIEW

Lifeguards and *swimming instructors* watch over and teach swimmers at public and private pools, beaches, health clubs, summer camps, private resorts, and public parks. Lifeguards enforce local laws and the particular regulations of their facility, and provide assistance to swimmers in need. One of their greatest responsibilities is preventing injuries and fatal accidents in or around water. Instructors hold group or individual swimming lessons. Most of their students are children, though instructors teach swimmers of all ages. Both lifeguards and instructors are trained professionals in the techniques of water rescue, cardiopulmonary resuscitation (CPR), and first aid.

HISTORY

Swimming was used first as a survival and hunting skill, then became a popular sporting event. Early hieroglyphics in Egyptian tombs dating from 2500–2000 B.C. depict human figures swimming. Around 78 A.D., swimming was introduced and promoted in England, and by the 14th century, knights were required to be able to swim in their full body armor. The Olympics included swimming as a sport in 1896 for men and 1912 for women.

As swimming grew in popularity as a form of recreation, people frequented local beaches and swimming pools. Soon, there arose a need for guards to patrol the waters and rescue swimmers in distress. There was also a need for certified instructors to teach new swimmers proper techniques to help them avoid emergencies in the first place.

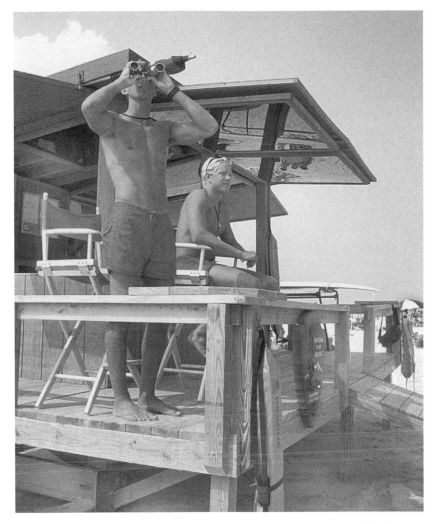

Lifeguards must watch over swimmers close to the shore and further out in the water. *(Gibson Stock Photography)*

The first lifeguards were loosely organized in groups similar to police or fire departments, and they were often employees of the local government. However, training was not standardized—guards used a variety of lifesaving methods. The 1956 Summer Olympics in Australia spotlighted the profession with an exhibition/competition of international lifesavers. As a result, techniques, experience, and equipment such as the rescue tube, rescue buoy, and surfboard, were introduced to lifeguards worldwide. Today, lifeguards must meet strict standards of physical condition, professional training and skill.

The *United States Lifesaving Association Manual of Open Water Lifesaving* is used by many as an important training guide.

Teaching techniques have also evolved over time. The dominating stroke for many years was the breaststoke, which was done with the head either in or out of the water, a side arm motion, and frog-like movement of the legs. Though this method of swimming was effective and thought to be graceful, it was not the fastest technique. In the mid 1950s, English amateur swimmer J. Arthur Trudgen took a trip to South America and noticed swimmers there with a different style. He brought the stroke back with him, calling it the Trudgen stroke, which, with changes from another competitive swimmer, Frederick Cavill, later became the still popular "crawl," or freestyle stroke. This technique, with arms moving up and over the head and legs kicking in a scissor-like motion, was soon used in competition and broke records of all distances. This freestyle stroke, along with the backstroke, the breaststroke, and the butterfly, are the main swimming techniques that instructors teach today.

THE JOB

Lifeguards patrol beaches, lakes, swimming pools, and other water areas to ensure safety of the patrons and management of the facility. Lifeguards monitor water activities to make sure all swimmers are safe. If swimmers go too far from shore or leave the designated swimming zone, the lifeguard is responsible for signaling the swimmer back to safer waters. In some cases, the lifeguard must physically bring the swimmer back. They also watch for any roughhousing in the water, as this may cause potential danger and injury. Lifeguards who are posted at lakes and ocean beaches must be on the watch for strong currents, changing weather conditions, and dangerous animals, such as jellyfish or sharks.

Lifeguards also enforce local laws or facility regulations. They must notify patrons if they are breaking beach rules such as drinking alcoholic beverages, using glass containers, swimming with pets, or driving motorized vehicles. Swimming pools usually ban similar items; some pools also enforce certain time periods based on age.

Lifeguards keep watch from tower stations, or elevated chairs. The height is advantageous because it allows the lifeguard clear visibility of the facility, as well as keeping the station in the public's view. Whistles, megaphones, and binoculars are helpful tools for maintaining order. Lifeguards also use equipment, such as floatation devices, ropes, poles, and small boats, during rescue attempts.

Lifeguards must be well versed in CPR and other first-aid techniques—such knowledge may mean the difference between life and death with drowning victims. They not only need to be strong swimmers, but they must be levelheaded, calm, and ready to react in emergency situations.

Many lifeguards also work as swimming instructors. Instructors are hired by public pools, private swim clubs, and schools to teach proper swimming techniques. Instructors generally teaching children or young adults, showing these students how to swim using different stokes and breathing techniques. They also may teach students how to rescue or resuscitate swimmers during emergencies.

REQUIREMENTS

High School
Most facilities require their lifeguards and instructors to have a high school diploma, or a GED equivalent. High school classes in physical education (especially swimming) and health will be helpful for this career.

Postsecondary Training
If you aspire to hold a pool or beach management position, such as pool manager or instructor supervisor, or to use your swimming training in a related career, then it would be wise to work toward a college degree. Consider degrees in health, recreation, or business.

Certification or Licensing
All lifeguards and instructors must be certified to work. Depending on their skill level, lifeguards must pass a training program, from basic lifeguard training to head lifeguard to aquatic professional. The basic lifeguard course lasts approximately six days and tests swimming skills. You will need to be able to swim 500 yards (no time frame) and tread water for one minute—as well as demonstrate your physical endurance, professionalism, and skills in using lifesaving equipment and techniques, CPR, and first aid. Head lifeguard courses teach advanced techniques in injury prevention, selection and training of guards, team building, and emergency response planning. To successfully complete the program, guards must attend and participate in the course, pass a written test, and demonstrate their guarding skills in the pool.

Instructors also must obtain certification to prove their teaching and swimming skills. The American Red Cross offers the designation Water Safety Instructor to individuals 17 years of age or older. To earn this designation, candidates must attend and participate in the course, pass a written test, and prove their skills in techniques such as shallow and deep water diving, rescue and lifesaving techniques, and demonstrate ability in all swimming strokes.

Other Requirements

Most training and certification programs require applicants to be at least 15 years of age. You should be in excellent physical condition, trustworthy, and able to exercise good judgment in serious situations. These jobs come with a tremendous amount of responsibility. Lifeguards are relied upon to keep water patrons safe and maintain order at their facility. Instructors are trusted with groups of small children who are not yet skilled at swimming.

EXPLORING

If you are interested in lifeguarding, the United States Lifesaving Association offers junior lifeguard programs to students aged nine to 17. Participants learn water and beach safety and first aid techniques, as well as build self-confidence in the water.

Another way to explore these careers is by talking to lifeguards and instructors at your local pool or beach. Ask them how they got their jobs and learned their swimming and guarding techniques. They may recommend certain programs for you to explore further.

EMPLOYERS

Lakes and beaches are not the only work venues for lifeguards and swimming instructors. Hotels, schools, park districts, and health clubs all have swimming facilities, as well as public pools and institutions, such as the YMCA. Most places hire lifeguards and instructors on a temporary or seasonal basis. Opportunities for full-time employment are greater in areas that have warm weather year round.

STARTING OUT

There is no standard way to enter this field. Many lifeguards and instructors find employment at facilities they normally frequent, or by word of mouth. The newspaper want ads are a good source— check under "Swimming Instructor" or "Lifeguard." Also, consider compiling a list of swimming facilities in your area and send job inquiries to those that interest you.

ADVANCEMENT

Many guards and instructors are employed on a temporary or seasonal basis, and they return to their jobs every summer until they finish school. There are quite a number of lifeguards and instructors who use their passion for the water and skills acquired while on the job as a basis for a full-time career. Dave Zielinski is a perfect example—he worked many summers as a lifeguard for his local YMCA. Today, he is employed as a Customer Service Support Manager for the Chicago chapter of the American Red Cross. Says Zielinski, "Lifeguarding gives an exciting avenue for those who enjoy the water."

There are other options as well. With hard work, ample experience, and further education, lifeguards and instructors can move into managerial positions such as *head lifeguard,* who assists managers and oversees all other guards; *aquatics manager,* who is responsible for the maintenance and operation of a pool; or *instructor supervisor,* who is involved in the hiring, training, and managing of all staff instructors. Highly skilled swimmers may choose to work as *aquatic specialists,* who run lifeguarding and instructor training programs or may even train professional swimmers.

EARNINGS

Earnings vary depending on several factors—facility or venue, hours worked, and certification status of the individual. According to a Florida lifeguard certification program, graduates of levels I and II earn between $6.50 and $7.21 an hour. Lifeguard I is considered a seasonal or temporary appointment, while Lifeguard II is a permanent position. Senior lifeguards earn between $9.21 and $13.80 an hour. Lifeguard supervisors are paid $11.75–$17.62 an hour.

Instructors may be paid per hour or per class. In general, they earn more for giving private lessons than teaching group sessions. According to a job posting on the summer employment website for the city of Salina, Kansas, instructor/lifeguards can earn between $6.50 and $7.50 per hour.

Full-time employees are often offered a benefits package consisting of paid vacation time, sick leave, health insurance, and a retirement plan.

WORK ENVIRONMENT

Work in the sun, surf, and the outdoors may be the ideal work atmosphere for some. However, these jobs are anything but easy. Lifeguards have a tremendous amount of responsibility when on duty. They must always be ready to prevent accidents and react quickly during emergencies, while resisting the distractions of the job environment. Similarly, instructors have to stay alert while teaching, especially when instructing young children. Instructors also have the added stress of teaching young students who may not enjoy their time in the pool, and as a result, may not cooperate or be on their best behavior.

Though instructors teach classes of varying lengths, most lifeguards work eight-hour shifts. Depending on the size of the facility, guards work in pairs or teams. "Expect long hours in the sun," says Dave Zielinski—especially if you are stationed outdoors.

OUTLOOK

The outlook for lifeguards and instructors is mixed. Public interest in health and physical fitness is increasing steadily. Also, water amusement parks, a collection of swimming pools, wave pools and water slides, are gaining popularity. Combined with lakes, beaches, private and public swimming pools, not to mention pools located within high schools and universities, the opportunity for employment is plentiful. However, most lifeguard and instructor positions are part time or seasonal, mainly lasting through the summer months. There are some swimming facilities open year round, though these jobs are rare. Many students take lifeguard or instructor positions to supplement their income until they finish school. Those who desire to have a full-time career as a lifeguard or instructor should seek the best training available and consider a college education, as well as advanced training in swimming and lifesaving procedures and techniques.

FOR MORE INFORMATION

For information regarding certification, education, or class schedules, contact
The American Red Cross
2025 E Street, NW
Washington, DC 20006
Tel: 202-303-4498
http://www.redcross.org

For information on careers, certification, or the junior lifeguard program, contact
United States Lifesaving Association
PO Box 9009

San Diego, CA 92169-0009
http://www.usla.org

For industry information, tryouts, or job descriptions, contact
US Ocean Safety
31131 Pacific Coast Highway
Laguna Beach, CA 92651
Tel: 949-443-0773
http://www.usos.com

Motivational Speakers

School Subjects
English
Speech

Personal Skills
Communication/ideas
Helping/teaching

Work Environment
Primarily indoors
Primarily multiple locations

Minimum Education Level
High school diploma

Salary Range
$100/speech to
$1,000/speech to
$2,500/speech

Certification or Licensing
Recommended

Outlook
About as fast as the average

DOT
N/A

GOE
N/A

NOC
N/A

O*NET-SOC
N/A

OVERVIEW

Motivational speakers give inspirational and informative speeches to groups of people. They are hired by businesses, schools, resorts, and communities to speak on topics such as achieving personal or financial success, living a healthy lifestyle, or organizing one's personal life or business. Speakers must tailor their message to their audience, whether it is a class of high school students or a group of business executives.

HISTORY

Motivation is the internal drive that urges people to act in a certain way. People are motivated through the expectation of a reward, whether tangible (such as a cash bonus) or intangible (such as internal satisfaction). People can also be motivated by fear of the loss of privileges or power (such as employment termination).

Throughout history, people have been motivated by different factors. During tough economic periods, people are motivated by money or even food. In good times, people are still motivated by money, but they can also find motivation in achieving intangible things such as success or publicity.

Though motivational speaking may seem like a recent invention, speakers have long been influencing people. For example, through their powerful speeches, political leaders such as Abraham Lincoln and Martin Luther King, Jr. motivated many people to act in certain ways.

A more recent development is the hiring of motivational speakers to inspire smaller and more specific audiences, such as sports teams. Whether motivational speakers are addressing a group of employees about improving job performance, or talking to a graduating class of college students about making it in the real world, their ultimate goal is the same: to motivate.

THE JOB

Motivational speakers are hired to speak on a variety of topics, depending on their audience and specialty. They may talk about overcoming alcohol or drug abuse, achieving athletic success, developing business skills, coping with change, communicating with others, working with computers, welcoming diversity, dealing with gender issues, protecting self-esteem, negotiating with a boss, improving performance, weight loss, handling relationships, adjusting to retirement/aging, or managing stress, just to name a few. Many speakers talk about how they overcame an obstacle and how others can do the same. They speak to young students, single parents, business professionals, athletes, school administrators, or any other group looking for advice and motivation.

Speakers need to worry about more than just delivering their speech. They have to prepare for the talk weeks or even months in advance, rehearsing their delivery and pinpointing their message to their specific audience.

On the day of their speech, motivational speakers should arrive at the location of their speech early to make sure that that everything is in place. Some speakers like to use microphones, while others are able to project their voice without using one. Some motivational speakers like to walk around while speaking and may require a cordless microphone, while others are more comfortable standing at a podium. All these details have to be worked out in advance to make sure the speech goes smoothly.

Speaking in public is something many people dislike, even fear, doing. But motivational speakers have to speak in front of audiences large and small on a regular basis. They have to sound confident, knowledgeable, and compassionate. They must make any performance fears that they have work for them—adding energy to their speech instead of nervousness.

Most importantly, motivational speakers must be engaging. Speakers shouldn't speak *to* their audience, they should speak *with* them. Everyone has faced hardships in life. For this reason, motivational speakers must try to relate to their audience members' experiences on some level. While speaking about overcoming obstacles such as depression, drug abuse, joblessness, or a losing streak, speakers may use funny, touching, or shocking stories from their own lives to connect with their listeners.

REQUIREMENTS

High School

Motivational speakers should have a high school diploma at the very least. Obvious class choices should include English and speech, but drama, foreign language, and computer classes would also be useful. Depending on what topic you wish to speak on, you could also take classes in business, history, science, or math—practically any area about which you feel passionately.

Postsecondary Training

A communications degree, though not required, would be useful for a job in public speaking. Advanced classes in speech, writing, and English will help you hone your communication skills and make you a stronger, more confident speaker. Again, depending on your specialty, you could also major in business, finance, political science, or other subject areas, but be sure to take communications classes on the side.

Certification or Licensing

To increase their credibility and marketing appeal, many motivational speakers seek certification to demonstrate their skills and experience. The National Speakers Association offers the Certified Speaking Professional (CSP) designation to professional speakers with many years of experience making money from speeches. Applicants must meet high standards, including certain educational requirements, having five years of public speaking experience, giving at least 250 presentations to audiences of 15 or more, working for at least 100 clients, and earning an annual average salary of $50,000 from speaking alone. The association also gives the title CSP candidate to individuals who have met some of these standards and are working toward full certification.

Other Requirements

Motivational speakers must be very confident in order to be able to speak in front of an audience. Besides being good communicators, speakers need to be able to connect with their listeners on a personal level. They should be compassionate and understanding and maintain a positive outlook on life. To be able to motivate and inspire others, they must be motivated and inspiring themselves! For their stories to be believable, speakers have to be honest about their experiences and not be afraid to share sometimes vulnerable moments in order to get their message across.

When Speaking in Front of a Crowd . . .

1. Know your environment. If possible, check out the room and any equipment you may use in advance. This way, there will be no surprises when you begin.

2. Know your crowd. Introduce yourself to members of the audience before you speak. This way, you'll know some of those faces staring back at you, and they may relate to your message more after having met you.

3. Know your stuff. This may sound obvious, but the more comfortable you are with your speech, the less nervous you'll be. Practice, practice, practice.

4. Know that people like you. Believe it or not, most people do not want to see you fail. Always think that the audience is on your side.

5. Breathe. Try to stay relaxed to make your speech sound natural and comfortable.

6. Don't be sorry. If you slip up or admit you're nervous, you're only hurting yourself. Keep the audience's attention on your message, not your mistakes.

7. Concentrate on your message, not your speaking ability. If you focus on the meaning of your speech instead of the (sometimes scary) act of speaking in public, your nervousness should decrease.

8. Visualize. Imagine yourself giving a successful speech, and you have a better chance of achieving it.

9. Channel nervous energy to help you. Use any mild nervousness to add vitality and energy to your speech.

10. Consider all speaking opportunities—even shaky ones—as good experience. You can gain knowledge from your mistakes as well as your successes as a speaker.

EXPLORING

To get a sense of what this career is like, you should take advantage of public speaking opportunities while in school. Participate in school plays to gain experience and skills performing in front of an audience. If your school has a speech or debate team, join and work on your speaking and debate skills. You will have to prepare your own argument and deliver it in front of people, including judges that are evaluating your delivery, use of eye contact, and overall performance.

Read magazines such as *Professional Speaker* to learn about hot topics and developments within the profession. Sample articles

are available on the National Speakers Association's website at
http://www.nsaspeaker.org.

EMPLOYERS

Motivational speakers are hired by a variety of clients. Depending on
the focus of their speeches, they are hired by schools, government
agencies, small businesses, large corporations, resorts, health clubs,
spas, and even cruise ships.

Most are self-employed and work for clients on a one-time basis.
Some speakers have repeat clients, such as speakers who are hired to
give a presentation at an annual conference. Speakers who focus on
employee training may be hired full time to train new workers directly or teach managers about training methods.

STARTING OUT

It is difficult to work full time as a motivational speaker. Most speakers work part time until they develop a list of clients and build a solid
reputation as a speaker. To start out, many speakers offer to talk for
free or for a nominal fee. This will give them experience and references for future clients.

Most speakers prepare promotional packets to send out to potential clients. These include an introductory letter, a resume, references,
a color photo, and a "demo" videotape of one of their speeches.

Clients also may choose to join a professional organization such
as the American Speakers Bureau Corporation for exposure and job
assistance. Speakers are listed on the organization's website,
http://www.speakersbureau.com, by specialty and region.

ADVANCEMENT

Motivational speakers advance by working for larger clients, earning more money per speech, or working full time. Popular motivational speakers can advance by working more in the spotlight, hosting
radio or television programs, writing books, or running websites. A
good example of this type of personality is Dr. Phil McGraw, personal
growth specialist, speaker, writer, and now TV host.

EARNINGS

According to Mike Moore, motivational speaker and operator of a
website, *Speak for Profit* (http://www.speakforprofit.com), beginning speakers can expect to earn between $100 and $200 per speech,

in addition to reimbursement for any expenses incurred. Within a year, dedicated and talented speakers can earn $400–$1,000 per speech, $1,500–$2,000 for a longer seminar, and $2,000–$2,500 for a full day of speaking.

It is important to note that earnings can be sporadic and depend wholly on the ability of the speaker to find clients and appointments.

WORK ENVIRONMENT

Motivational speakers work in a variety of locations, from business boardrooms to school cafeterias. They generally speak indoors but may work outdoors on occasion, such as during a graduation ceremony.

When not "talking," speakers generally work from home, gathering information for their next assignment and looking for new business opportunities.

While giving speeches, motivational speakers work in what many may consider a stressful environment, with hundreds and maybe thousands of people watching and listening. But to the successful motivational speaker, this environment is viewed as thrilling and captivating.

OUTLOOK

Membership in the National Speakers Association has increased by 30 percent in the last decade, indicating growth in the speaking profession. However, the job market for motivational speakers depends on their specialty and targeted audiences. Those who speak at schools are affected by budget cuts that can make the hiring of professional speakers a financial impossibility. Those who speak to professional associations, however, are seeing growth in the number of job opportunities available. According to a recent study by the American Society of Association Executives, nearly half of all seminars and three-fourths of all conventions hosted by associations include a professional speaker as part of their scheduling.

Because of the nature of the job, motivational speakers will always find opportunities to impart their wisdom. However, like other self-employed workers, it's the speaker's resourcefulness and marketability that will determine his or her success.

FOR MORE INFORMATION

To learn more about this professional association of speakers on a variety of topics, contact
American Speakers Bureau Corporation
10151 University Boulevard, #197

Orlando, FL 32817
Tel: 407-826-4248
Email: info@speakersbureau.com
http://www.speakersbureau.com

For information about certification and training programs, contact
National Speakers Association
1500 South Priest Drive
Tempe, AZ 85281
Tel: 480-968-2552
http://www.nsaspeaker.org

For information on membership and other resources for speakers in Canada, contact
Canadian Association of Professional Speakers
39 River Street
Toronto, ON M5A 3P1 Canada
Tel: 416-646-1600
Email: info@canadianspeakers.org
http://www.canadianspeakers.org

Personal Trainers

OVERVIEW

Personal trainers, often known as *fitness trainers,* assist health-conscious people with exercise, weight training, weight loss, diet and nutrition, and medical rehabilitation. During one training session, or over a period of several sessions, trainers teach their clients how to achieve their health and fitness goals. They train in the homes of their clients, their own studio spaces, or in health clubs. More than 62,000 personal trainers work in the United States, either independently or on the staff of a fitness center.

HISTORY

For much of the last half of the 20th century, "98-pound weaklings" were tempted by the Charles Atlas comic book ads to buy his workout plan and to bulk up. Atlas capitalized on a concern for good health that developed into the fitness industry after World War II. Though physical fitness has always been important to the human body, things have changed quite a bit since the days when people had to chase and hunt their own food. Before the industrial revolution, people were much more active, and the need for supplemental exercise was unnecessary. But the last century has brought easier living, laziness, and processed snack foods.

Even as early as the late 1800s, people became concerned about their health and weight and began to flock to spas and exercise camps. This proved to be a passing fad for the most part, but medical and nutritional experts began to explore the significance of exercise. During World War II, rehabilitation medicine proved more effective than extended rest in returning soldiers to the front line. Even the early days of TV featured many morning segments devoted to exercise. The videotape revolution

QUICK FACTS

School Subjects
Health
Physical education

Personal Skills
Communication/ideas
Helping/teaching

Work Environment
Primarily indoors
Primarily multiple locations

Minimum Education Level
Some postsecondary training

Salary Range
$20/hour to $40/hour to
$100/hour

Certification or Licensing
Voluntary

Outlook
Faster than the average

DOT
153

GOE
N/A

NOC
N/A

O*NET-SOC
29-9091.00

of the 1980s went hand in hand with a new fitness craze, as Jane Fonda's workout tape became a bestseller and inspired a whole industry of fitness tapes and books. Now most health clubs offer the services of personal trainers to attend to the health and fitness concerns of its members.

THE JOB

Remember the first time you ever went to the gym? The weight machines may have resembled medieval forms of torture. So, to avoid the weight training, you stuck to the treadmill. Or maybe you called upon the services of a personal trainer. Personal trainers help their clients achieve health and fitness goals. They instruct on the proper use of exercise equipment and weight machines and may suggest diet and nutrition tips.

If you've reached your own workout goals, then you may be ready to help others reach theirs. "You have to believe in working out and eating healthy," advises Emelina Edwards, a personal trainer in New Orleans. For 12 years she's been in the business of personal training, a career she chose after whipping herself into great shape at the age of 46. Now, at 58, she has a lot of first-hand experience in training, nutrition, aerobic exercise, and stress management. Edwards says, "You have to practice what you preach."

And practice Edwards does—not only does she devote time every day to her own weight training, jogging, and meditation, but she works with three to five clients in the workout facility in her home. She has a total of about 20 clients, some of whom she assists in one-on-one sessions, and others in small groups. Her clients have included men and women from the ages of 20 to 80 who are looking to improve their general physical condition or to work on specific ailments.

When meeting with a client for the first time, Edwards gets a quick history of his or her physical problems and medical conditions. "If problems are serious," Edwards says, "I check with their doctor. If mild, I explain to them what I believe will help." When she discovered that four out of five people seeking her help suffered from back problems, she did a great deal of research on back pain and how to alleviate it through exercise. "I teach people how to do for themselves," she says. "Sometimes I see a person once, or for three or four sessions, or forever."

In addition to working directly with clients, Edwards is active promoting her line of "Total Body Rejuvenation" products. These products, consisting of audio tapes and books, are based on her years of experience and the many articles she has written for fitness publications. When she's not training clients, writing articles, and selling products, she's reading fitness publications to keep up on the business, as well as speaking at public events. "When I realized I loved training," she says, "I thought of all the things I could relate to it. So along with the training, I began to write about it, and to give talks on health and fitness."

Successful personal trainers don't necessarily have to keep as busy as Edwards. They may choose to specialize in certain areas of personal training. They may work as an *athletic trainer,* helping athletes prepare for sports activities. They may specialize in helping with the rehabilitation treatment of people with injuries and other physical problems. Yoga, dance, martial arts, indoor cycling, boxing, and water fitness have all become aspects of special training programs. People call upon personal trainers to help them quit smoking, to assist with healthy pregnancies, and to maintain mental and emotional stability. Whatever the problem, whether mental or physical, people are turning to exercise and nutrition to help them deal with it.

Many personal trainers have their own studios or home gyms where they train their clients; others go into the homes of their clients. Because of the demands of the workplace, many personal trainers also work in offices and corporate fitness centers. Though most health clubs hire their own trainers to assist with club members, some hire freelance trainers as independent contractors. These independent contractors are not considered staff members and don't receive employee benefits. (IDEA, a fitness professional association, found that 30 percent of the personal trainers hired by the fitness centers surveyed were independent contractors.)

REQUIREMENTS

High School
If you're interested in health and fitness, you're probably already taking physical education classes and involved in sports activities. It's also important to take health courses and courses like home economics, which include lessons in diet and nutrition. Business courses can help you prepare for the management aspect of running your own personal training service. Science courses such as biology, chemistry, and physiology are important for your understanding of muscle groups, food and drug reactions, and other concerns of exercise science. If you're not interested in playing on sports teams, you may be able to volunteer as an assistant. These positions will allow you to learn about athletic training as well as rehabilitation treatments.

Postsecondary Training
A college education isn't required to work as a personal trainer, but you can benefit from one of the many fitness-related programs offered at colleges across the country. Some relevant college programs include

health education, exercise and sports science, fitness program management, and athletic training. These programs include courses in therapeutic exercise, nutrition, aerobics, and fitness and aging. IDEA recommends a bachelor's degree from a program that includes at least a semester each in anatomy, kinesiology, and exercise physiology. IDEA has some scholarships available to students seeking careers as fitness professionals.

If you're not interested in a full four-year program, many schools offer shorter versions of their bachelor's programs. Upon completing a shorter program, you'll receive either an associate's degree or certification from the school. Once you've established yourself in the business, continuing education courses are important for you to keep up with the advances in the industry. IDEA is one of many organizations that offer independent study courses, conferences, and seminars.

Certification or Licensing

There are so many schools and organizations that offer certification to personal trainers that it has become a concern in the industry. Without more rigid standards, the profession could suffer at the hands of less experienced, less skilled trainers. Some organizations only require membership fees and short tests for certification. Emelina Edwards isn't certified and doesn't believe that certification is necessary. "Experience is what counts," she says.

But some health clubs look for certified trainers when hiring independent contractors. If you are seeking certification, you should choose a certifying board that offers scientifically based exams and requires continuing education credits. The American Council on Exercise, the National Federation of Professional Trainers, and the American Fitness Professionals and Associates are just a few of the many groups with certification programs.

Other Requirements

Physical fitness and knowledge of health and nutrition are the most important assets of personal trainers. "The more intelligently you can speak to someone," Edwards says, "the more receptive they'll be." Your clients will also be more receptive to patience and friendliness. "I'm very enthusiastic and positive," she says regarding the way she works with her clients. You should be able to explain things clearly, recognize progress, and encourage it. You should be comfortable working one-on-one with people of all ages and in all physical conditions. An interest in reading fitness books and publications is important to your continuing education.

EXPLORING

Your high school may have a weight-training program, or some other extracurricular fitness program, as part of the athletic department—in addition to signing up for the program, assist the faculty who manage it. That way, you can learn about what goes into developing and maintaining such a program. If your school doesn't have a fitness program, seek one out at a community center, or join a health club.

You should also try the services of a personal trainer. By conditioning yourself and eating a healthy diet, you'll get a good sense of the duties of a personal trainer. Any number of books and magazines address issues of health and nutrition and offer weight training advice. One helpful publication, *IDEA Personal Trainer,* is published 10 times a year.

Finally, seek out part-time work at a gym or health club to meet trainers and learn about weight machines and certification programs.

EMPLOYERS

IDEA reports that there are more than 62,000 personal trainers working in the United States. Personal trainers are employed by people of all ages. Individuals hire the services of trainers, as do companies for the benefit of their employees. Though most health clubs hire personal trainers full time, some clubs hire trainers on an independent contractor basis. Sports and exercise programs at community colleges hire trainers part time to conduct classes.

Personal trainers can find clients in most major cities in all regions of the country. In addition to health clubs and corporate fitness centers, trainers find work at YMCAs, aerobics studios, and hospital fitness centers.

STARTING OUT

Most people who begin personal training do so after successful experiences with their own training. Once they've developed a good exercise regimen and healthy diet plan for themselves, they may feel ready to help others. Emelina Edwards had hit a low point in her life, following a divorce and money problems, and had turned to weight training to help her get through the difficult times. "I didn't have a college degree," she says, "and I needed something to do. All I had was weight training." She then called up all the women she knew, promoting her services as a personal trainer. Through the benefit of word-of-mouth, Edwards built up a clientele.

Some trainers begin by working part time or full time for health clubs and, after making connections, they go into business for themselves. As with most small businesses, personal trainers must promote themselves through classified ads, flyers posted in community centers, and other forms of advertisement. Many personal trainers have published guides on how to establish businesses. IDEA offers a package called *The Business of Personal Training: How to Manage Growth and Profitability,* which includes a textbook and audio cassettes with advice on selling and marketing services, developing networking skills, and creating partnerships with retailers, medical professionals, and others.

ADVANCEMENT

After personal trainers have taken on as many individual clients as they need to maintain a business, they may choose to lead small group training sessions or conduct large aerobics classes. Some trainers join forces with other trainers to start their own fitness centers. Trainers who are employed by fitness centers may be promoted to the position of *personal training director.* These workers supervise and schedule other personal trainers and manage department budgets.

Emelina Edwards has advanced her business by venturing out into other areas of fitness instruction, such as publishing books and speaking to groups. "I want to develop more in the public speaking arena," she says. Right now, she only speaks to local groups—she'd like to go national.

EARNINGS

A compensation survey conducted by IDEA in 2000 reports that personal trainers who worked for health clubs and other fitness centers earned an average of $23 an hour. The top four factors determining pay were degree/certification, specialty area expertise, continuing education, and years in the industry. Personal trainers who offer specialized instruction (such as in yoga, martial arts, or indoor cycling) earned an average of $20 an hour. Personal training directors, who supervise other personal trainers, earned an annual salary of $25,500.

Personal trainers who work with their own clients in their own homes can charge a higher hourly rate. The average hourly fee for the services of personal trainers ranges from $40 to $100.

WORK ENVIRONMENT

Personal training is obviously a physically demanding job, but anybody who is in good shape and who eats a healthy diet should be able to easily handle the demands. Personal trainers who work out of their homes will enjoy familiar and comfortable surroundings. Trainers who work in a gym as independent contractors will also experience a comfortable workplace. Most good gyms maintain a cool temperature, keep the facilities clean and well lit, and care for the weight machines. Whether in a gym or at home, personal trainers work directly with their clients, usually in one-on-one training sessions. In this teaching situation, the workplace is usually quiet and conducive to learning.

As with most self-employment, sustaining a business can be both rewarding and difficult. Many trainers appreciate being able to keep their own hours, and to work as little, or as much, as they care to. By setting their own schedules, they can arrange time for their personal workout routines. But, without an employer, there's less security, no benefits, and no steady paycheck. Personal trainers have to regularly promote their services and be ready to take on new clients.

OUTLOOK

Fitness training will continue to enjoy strong growth in the near future. As the baby boomers grow older, they will increasingly rely on the services of personal trainers. Boomers have long been interested in health and fitness, and they'll carry this into their old age. A knowledge of special weight training, stretching exercises, and diets for seniors will be necessary for personal trainers in the years to come. Trainers will actively promote their services to senior centers and retirement communities.

With the number of health publications and fitness centers, people are much more knowledgeable about exercise and nutrition. This could increase business for personal trainers as people better understand the necessity of proper training and seek out professional assistance. Trainers may also be going into more of their clients homes as people set up their own workout stations complete with weights and treadmills. In the health and medical field, new developments are constantly affecting how people eat and exercise. Personal trainers must keep up with these advances, as well as any new trends in fitness and dieting.

FOR MORE INFORMATION

For general health and fitness topics, and to learn about certification, contact
American Council on Exercise
4851 Paramount Drive
San Diego, CA 92123
Tel: 800-825-3636
http://www.acefitness.org

For information on certification, contact
American Fitness Professionals and Associates
PO Box 214
Ship Bottom, NJ 08008
Tel: 609-978-7583
Email: afpa@afpafitness.com
http://www.afpafitness.com

IDEA conducts surveys, provides continuing education, and publishes a number of books and magazines relevant to personal trainers. For information about the fitness industry in general, and personal training specifically, contact
IDEA, Inc.
6190 Cornerstone Court East, #204
San Diego, CA 92121-3773
Email: nonmemberquestions@ideafit.com
http://www.ideafit.com

For information on certification, contact
National Federation of Professional Trainers
PO Box 4579
Lafayette, IN 47903
Tel: 800-729-6378
Email: info@nfpt.com
http://www.nfpt.com

──────────── **INTERVIEW** ────────────

Chris Neubauer is a personal trainer at an athletic club in Chicago. With many triathlons under his belt, he often works with triathletes preparing for competition, in addition to working with general members looking for assistance with their exercise programs. Neubauer spoke to the editors of Careers in Focus: Coaches & Fitness Professionals *about his job and training.*

Q. Please describe your job duties.
A. I create fitness programs for people of all levels and conditions: triathletes, post-rehabilitation patients, individuals with spinal disorders, pregnant women, etc. I give clients nutritional and lifestyle advice and sometimes check in with them throughout the year to make sure that they're on track.

Q. What is your work environment like?

A. I work at three health clubs and work with a few clients in their homes. When training triathletes, I sometimes work outdoors, planning their workouts on the lakefront path.

Q. How did you train for this job? What was your college major?

A. I actually never took a college course on fitness—my college major was psychology and speech disorders. I was kind of *pushed* into this career by some co-workers who thought I'd be good at it. I took their advice and signed up for college courses, seminars, and conferences to prepare myself.

Q. If you could start your education all over again, what would you do?

A. I would now choose to pursue physical therapy (PT) because I think the body is such an amazing entity. It heals itself! I think PT interests me the most because I could work to help people deal with and overcome injuries.

Q. How/where did you get your first job in this field? What did you do?

A. I started out cleaning toilets and answering the phones at a gym called ROBIX in Chicago. There was only one personal trainer employed there at the time, and because I was interested in fitness, management asked me if I was interested in training people. I learned as much as I could and started to pick up clients. Once I started, the clients just kept coming.

Q. What kind of sources are available to someone looking to get into this field?

A. Many websites offer useful information about training and education options. For example, the C.H.E.K. Institute (http://www.chek-institute.com), the National Academy of Sports Fitness (http://www.nasm.org), and the American Council on Exercise (http://www.acefitness.org) all offer resources for fitness professionals. I also know of many universities that now offer majors in the sports and fitness field.

Q. What are the most important personal and professional qualities for personal trainers?

A. I think you have to love what you do. If not, you won't make it. Many times, the thought of money from this job *never* enters my mind. Instead, what matters to me most is the smile on my clients' face when they've lost anywhere from two to 50 pounds, they made it one week without candy, or they can walk a mile without tiring.

However, you have to be sure to know your limits. Be aware of when to refer a client to another professional. Trying to act "smooth" by pretending to know everything there is to know can really screw up a training relationship.

Q. What are some of the pros and cons of your job?

A. Some of the cons include occasional sleep deprivation, choosing your clients' health over your own, and working on the weekends. But this career is fun, it's healthy, and it keeps you young!

Q. What is the most important piece of advice that you have to offer students as they graduate and look for jobs in this field?

A. If you really care about people, try it out, but promise yourself and your clients that you'll do everything to further your education. You need to be able to give them the most up-to-date and no-nonsense exercise programs to further their health and fitness.

Physical Education Teachers

OVERVIEW

Physical education (PE) teachers instruct students in kindergarten through grade 12 about physical fitness and health. They may organize physical education programs for an entire school or just a few classes. PE teachers make up only a small percentage of the over 4 million teachers employed in the United States.

HISTORY

In the United States, organized physical education is less than 200 years old. In 1823, George Bancroft, an historian and statesman, opened the Round Hill School in Northampton, Massachusetts. In 1825, Bancroft hired Charles Beck to teach Latin and physical education. Beck, a follower of Friedrich Ludwig Jahn, a German known as the "Father of Gymnastics," is often considered to be the first physical education teacher in the United States. Amherst College in Massachusetts opened the first department of physical education in the United States in 1860. One year later, the physician Dioclesian Lewis founded the Normal Institute of Physical Education in Boston, Massachusetts. It was the first school to prepare teachers of physical education. Following the Civil War, physical education became part of many educational programs.

In the early 20th century, physical education programs expanded and improved rapidly. Between 1901 and 1925, 32 states passed physical education legislation requiring some sort of physical training in schools.

By the early 1950s, fitness tests revealed that American children were lagging behind their European counterparts. In response, President Eisenhower formed the Council on Youth Fitness, which ultimately became the President's Council on Physical Fitness and Sports. Physical fitness programs grew in popularity in schools. They focused largely on activities that developed athletic skills, such as calisthenics and competitive sports.

During the past two decades, physical education classes have been under attack by school systems interested in saving money and improving academic performance in traditional academic disciplines. The introduction of classes such as computer science, art, foreign language, and music into school curriculums has also reduced the time allotted for physical education classes.

According to the National Association for Sport and Physical Education, only about half of K–12 students and only 29 percent of high school students have physical education classes daily. In 2001, only 25 percent of all students attended a PE class, according to the Centers for Disease Control (CDC)—down from 42 percent of students in 1991. Illinois is the only state in the nation that requires daily PE, but, since 1995, Illinois schools have been allowed to seek waivers to exempt them from compliance.

These reductions in physical education programs have contributed to an increasing epidemic of overweight and obese children. Nine million children and teens ages six to 19 are overweight—a 300 percent increase since 1980, according to the U.S. Department of Health and Human Services. The CDC reports that 13.6 percent of children are obese—an increase of nearly 9 percent from 30 years ago. Health problems for overweight and obese children include heart disease, high cholesterol, high blood pressure, and the development of type 2 diabetes (a disease previously limited to adults).

Ironically, studies have shown clear links between athletic fitness and academic success. A 2001 study by the California Department of Education found a strong relationship between academic achievement and the physical fitness of students in its public schools. Reading and mathematics scores were matched with the fitness scores of nearly 1 million fifth-, seventh-, and ninth-grade students. The fittest students had higher academic achievement levels, especially in mathematics.

Physical education classes today focus on the development of fitness skills, nonathletic competition, individual exercise goals, and aerobic training. This new approach to physical education is often referred to as "the new PE." Madison Junior High School in Naperville, Illinois, is an excellent model of how the new PE is changing the lives of young people. While kids at Madison still participate in team sports during gym class, PE instructors also teach them how to use exercise bikes, weights, inline skates, and treadmills. The school even has a rock-climbing wall that students can use. According to an article on the CNN Student News website, Madison students are graded on how well they stay within heart-rate zones rather than who runs the fastest. Students also receive a computer printout that records their heart rate, body fat, and cholesterol levels. Students are tracked through the 12th grade. Approximately 30 percent of schools in Illinois have changed to this new physical education model.

Public officials are beginning to see the value of physical education in the schools. Congress passed The Physical Education for Progress Act in 2000. It authorizes the Secretary of Education to award grants to school districts to start, expand, and improve K–12 physical education programs. Grants may be used to purchase athletic equipment, develop curriculum, and hire and train physical education staff.

As a result of this legislation and continuing lobbying efforts by physical education advocacy organizations, PE teachers can expect an optimistic employment outlook for their field.

THE JOB

Physical education teachers, through participation in individual and team sports, lectures, and other activities, educate students about fitness, nutrition, and general health. They use their knowledge of sports techniques and human physiology to develop exercise plans for students at the kindergarten through high school levels. Physical education programs not only develop the physical abilities of students but also help them to develop personal attributes such as self-discipline, sportsmanship, judgment, communication skills, teamwork, self-confidence, self-esteem, and the ability to set and meet goals. PE teachers may work alone or with one or more PE teachers and may be employed at more than one school.

According to the Council of Physical Education for Children, physical education teachers use different methods of instruction based on the age of their students. *Elementary school physical education teachers* use educational games, basic dance, gymnastics, and other activities to help their students develop important motor skills such as throwing, jumping, skipping, hopping, kicking, and catching. Instructors at this level usually teach eight to 10 classes daily, which are generally 30 minutes each.

Middle school students require a more systematic and structured approach to physical education. *Middle school physical education teachers* use traditional sports (such as volleyball and basketball), adventure activities (such as rock climbing, rope climbing, and skiing), and leisure activities (such as inline skating and biking) to help students stay fit. They set performance goals and assess the fitness levels of their students. Middle school PE instructors teach three to six classes daily. These classes last from 60 to 90 minutes.

High school students are much more physically, emotionally, and intellectually developed than elementary and middle school students. They are more likely to choose sports activities based on their own interests, and they take more responsibility for health and fitness choices. While continuing to educate students about traditional, adventure, and leisure activities, *high school physical education teachers* focus on helping students establish positive habits and attitudes about exercise and fitness. They help students explore and develop their specific sports and fitness interests with the hope that they will continue to remain fitness and health conscious during the rest of their lives. High school PE instructors teach three to six classes daily. These classes last from 60 to 90 minutes.

After each class, physical education teachers store equipment that was used during class. They order supplies and new equipment. They might also write up notes on how students performed during the class.

Outside of the gym or fitness center, physical education teachers prepare lesson plans and activities. They evaluate student work and calculate grades. In the process of planning their classes, PE teachers read fitness- and health-related magazines, books, and websites to learn more about their field. They practice exercises or fitness activities to be able to better demonstrate them to students. They also continue to study alternative and traditional teaching methods to hone their skills. PE teachers attend educational conferences to learn more about their field. They attend faculty meetings, parent-teacher conferences, and state and national teacher conferences. Many PE teachers have the opportunity for extracurricular work as athletic coaches. They also monitor students during lunch, break times, and study halls. They may accompany student groups on field trips and to competitions and events. High school PE teachers may be required to teach health classes as part of their duties.

Some physical education teachers are trained to teach those with disabilities. Special physical education is a federally mandated part of special education services. *Adapted physical education teachers* modify, adapt, and/or change a physical activity so that students with disabilities can do them. Disabilities include mental retardation, orthopedic impairment, speech or language impairment, attention deficit hyperactivity disorder, autism, behavioral disorders, cerebral palsy, visual impairments, hearing impairments, and learning disabilities.

REQUIREMENTS

High School

In addition to taking physical education and participating in as many sports as possible, take college preparatory classes, including mathematics, science, and psychology. You should also take speech and English courses to develop your communication skills.

Postsecondary Training

You will need to earn a minimum of a bachelor's degree in health and physical education to work as a physical education teacher. Typical classes for this major include exercise physiology, kinesiology, health and wellness, first aid/cardiopulmonary resuscitation (CPR), sports psychology, teaching physical education/health, and activity courses that teach the fundamentals of specific sports such as golf, aerobics, basketball, tennis, and track.

An advanced degree is usually required to teach physical education at the college level. Visit http://www.gradschools.com for a list of schools that offer graduate programs in sports and physical education.

There are over 500 accredited teacher education programs in the United States. Most of these programs are designed to meet the certificate requirements for the state in which they're located. Some states may require that you pass a test before being admitted to an educational program. You may choose to major in your subject area while taking required education courses, or you may major in secondary education with a concentration in your subject area. You'll probably have advisers (both in education and in your chosen specialty) to help you select courses.

In addition to a degree, a training period of student teaching in an actual physical education environment is usually required. Students are placed in schools to work with full-time teachers. During this period, undergraduate students observe the ways in which lessons are presented and the gym or fitness center is managed. Students also learn how to keep records of such details as attendance and grades and get actual experience in handling the class, both under supervision and alone.

Certification or Licensing

Voluntary teacher certification in physical education is available from the National Board for Professional Teaching Standards (NBPTS). Applicants must have a bachelor's degree and three years of classroom experience in a public or private school. They must prepare a portfolio of their teaching experience and complete exercises at an NBPTS assessment center to demonstrate their knowledge of their teaching specialty. After they complete these requirements and pay an application fee, they can use the designation National Board Certified Teacher (NBCT). Certifications are available in Early and Middle Childhood and Early Adolescence through Young Adulthood. Certification is valid for 10 years and is renewable. As of 2002, there were approximately 24,000 NBCTs employed in schools across the United States. For more information, visit http://www.nbpts.org/standards/nbcert.cfm.

The American Board for Certification of Teacher Excellence also offers voluntary certification. Prospective teachers can earn the Passport to Teaching Certification. Starting in 2004, experienced teachers will be able to earn the Master Teaching Certification. Contact http://www.abcte.org for more information.

The National Consortium for Physical Education and Recreation for Individuals with Disabilities offers a voluntary certification program for adapted physical education instructors. Instructors who pass an exam and meet other professional requirements may use the professional designation, Certified Adapted Physical Educator (CAPE). For more information on this certification, visit http://www.cortland.edu/apens.

Public school teachers must be licensed under regulations established by the department of education of the state in which they teach. Not all states require licensure for teachers in private or parochial schools. When you've received your teaching degree, you may request that a transcript of your college record be sent to the licensure section of your state department of education. If you have met licensure requirements, you will receive a certificate and thus be eligible to teach in the public schools of your state. In some states, you may have to take additional tests. If you move to another state, you will have to resubmit college transcripts, as well as comply with any other regulations in the new state, to be able to teach there.

Other Requirements

To be a successful PE teacher, you must be in good physical shape. You must have knowledge of human physiology and the psychological factors involved in physical education. You must also be willing to continue to learn about physical education and fitness and like helping children learn fitness techniques and maintain good overall health. You need strong interpersonal and instructional skills to be able to communicate well with students. You should also be well organized, as you'll have to keep track of the work and progress of many students.

Adolescence can be a troubling time for children, and these troubles often affect behavior and performance. This will require you to be very patient because children learn at different levels. You must also have good motivation skills to be able to properly motivate students who do not want to participate in class or perform up to appropriate levels. Because you'll be working with students who are at very impressionable ages, you should serve as a good role model.

EXPLORING

Consider ordering a student subscription to periodicals such as *Teaching Elementary Physical Education* and the *Journal of Teaching in Physical Education*. These publications, popular with PE teachers, will give you a useful overview of the field. Both of these publications can be ordered at the Human Kinetics Publishers website, http://www.humankinetics.com.

Becoming a student member of the American Alliance for Health, Physical Education, Recreation and Dance will allow you to access information on health and physical education as well as receive the periodicals *Strategies* and *The Journal of Physical Education, Recreation & Dance*. (See the contact information listed at the end of this chapter.)

By attending gym class, you've already gained a good sense of the daily work of a physical education teacher. But the requirements of a teacher go far beyond the gym or fitness center, so ask your PE teachers if you can talk with them after school. Interview your teachers about the amount of work that goes into preparing a class and directing activities. Look into coaching an athletic team, counseling at a summer camp, or working part time at a fitness center. This will give you experience coaching and interacting with young people.

EMPLOYERS

Physical education instructors are employed at public and private schools. They work in elementary schools, middle schools, junior high schools, high schools, junior colleges, and four-year universities. They are also employed by boys/girls clubs, camps, health spas and resorts, correctional facilities, martial arts studios, dance studios, resorts, community centers, child care facilities, fitness centers, health clubs, and gyms.

STARTING OUT

After completing your student teaching and becoming certified, you'll work with your college's placement office to find a full-time position. The departments of education of some states maintain listings of job openings. Many schools advertise teaching positions in the classified sections of major newspapers. You may also directly contact the principals and superintendents of the schools in which you'd like to work. While looking for full-time work, you can work as a substitute teacher. In urban areas with many schools, you may be able to substitute full time. PE Central, an organization for health and physical educators, also offers job listings for physical education teachers at its website, http://www.pecentral.org.

ADVANCEMENT

Most physical education teachers advance simply by becoming more of an expert in their field. They usually receive an increase in salary as they acquire experience. Additional training or study can also bring an increase in salary.

A few PE teachers who have management ability and an interest in administrative work may advance to the position of principal. Others may advance into supervisory positions or teach aspiring physical educators at colleges and universities. For most of these advanced positions, additional education is required. Some PE teachers also make lateral moves into other education-related positions such as guidance counselor.

Physical education instructors may choose to advance by working outside of the physical education field. With further education and experience, PE instructors can become exercise physiologists, sports trainers, sports nutritionists, fitness industry workers, coaches, and kinesiologists.

EARNINGS

The National Association of Colleges and Employers reports that the average starting offer for new graduates with a bachelor's degree in physical education teaching/coaching was $26,424 in 2003.

The U.S. Department of Labor reports that the median annual salary for elementary school teachers was $41,080 in 2001. The lowest paid 10 percent earned $27,000; the highest paid 10 percent earned $64,280 or more. Middle school teachers earned salaries that ranged from $27,790 to $64,270 in 2001. Secondary school teachers had median earnings of $43,280 in 2001. Ten percent earned less than $27,980, and 10 percent earned $67,940 or more annually.

In general, teachers who obtain certification receive higher salaries than teachers who are not certified.

Most teachers are contracted to work nine months out of the year, though some contracts are made for 10 months or a full year. In most cases, teachers have the option of prorating their salary up to 52 weeks. Teachers can also supplement their earnings through teaching summer classes, coaching sports, sponsoring a club, or other extracurricular work.

On behalf of teachers, unions bargain with schools over contract conditions such as wages, hours, and benefits. A majority of teachers join the American Federation of Teachers or the National Education Association. Depending on the state, teachers usually receive a retirement plan, sick leave, and health and life insurance. Some systems grant teachers sabbatical leave.

WORK ENVIRONMENT

Physical education teachers work in generally pleasant conditions. Some older schools may have poor heating and cooling systems. Instructors teach some classes outdoors in hot, cold, rainy, and other challenging weather conditions. School hours are generally 8 A.M. to 3 P.M., but all teachers work more than 40 hours a week teaching, preparing for classes, assessing grades, and directing extracurricular activities. As a coach or faculty adviser for an extracurricular activity, physical education instructors may have to work some evenings and weekends.

This job can be occasionally tiring and trying. Physical education instructors are on their feet for many hours each day explaining and demonstrating fitness activities. They must also handle disciplinary problems. Physical education instructors teach classes that are as small as 20 or fewer students or as large as 100–200 students. Some PE teachers may have to teach excessively large classes due to budget cuts and understaffing. This can lead to stress and burnout.

Students, parents, and school administrators may approach physical education with skepticism and a lack of respect. They may feel that PE is not as important an academic discipline as geometry, chemistry, or foreign language. PE teachers must be willing to educate these people regarding the benefits of proper fitness for children and discuss how modern physical education programs build life skills and reduce serious health problems in children.

Some physical education teachers who are employed at more than one school may have to travel back and forth between schools during their workdays.

OUTLOOK

Physical fitness is growing in popularity in the United States. The President's Council on Physical Fitness and Sports continues to encourage children and adults to be fit. A majority of adults and teens surveyed in 2000 by the National Association for Sport and Physical

Education feel that physical education should be mandatory in schools. Although physical education programs continue to be cut, there is hope that this renewed interest in exercise and fitness will reverse this trend. The U.S. Department of Education predicts average growth for preschool, elementary, middle, and secondary school teachers over the next several years.

FOR MORE INFORMATION

For information on student membership, contact
American Alliance for Health, Physical Education, Recreation
  and Dance
1900 Association Drive
Reston, VA 20191-1598
http://www.aahperd.org

For information on teacher certification, contact
American Board for Certification of Teacher Excellence
1225 19th Street, NW, Suite 400
Washington, DC 20036
Tel: 202-261-2620
Email: contact@abcte.org
http://www.abcte.org

For information about union membership, contact the following organizations:
American Federation of Teachers
555 New Jersey Avenue, NW
Washington, DC 20001
Tel: 202-879-4400
Email: online@aft.org
http://www.aft.org

National Education Association
1201 16th Street, NW
Washington, DC 20036
Tel: 202-833-4000
http://www.nea.org

For information on health issues for students and physical education teachers, contact
American School Health Association
7263 State Route 43

PO Box 708
Kent, OH 44240
Tel: 330-678-1601
Email: asha@ashaweb.org
http://www.ashaweb.org

For information on professional membership, contact
National Association for Sport and Physical Education
1900 Association Drive
Reston, VA 20191-1598
http://www.aahperd.org/naspe

For information on teacher certification, contact
National Board for Professional Teaching Standards
1525 Wilson Boulevard, Suite 500
Arlington, VA 22209
Tel: 703-465-2700
http://www.nbpts.org/nbct

For information on the CAPE designation, contact
National Consortium for Physical Education and Recreation for Individuals with Disabilities
Tel: 607-753-4969
Email: apens@cortland.edu
http://www.cortland.edu/apens

For information on accredited teacher education programs and teaching careers, contact
National Council for Accreditation of Teacher Education
2010 Massachusetts Avenue, NW, Suite 500
Washington, DC 20036-1023
Tel: 202-466-7496
Email: ncate@ncate.org
http://www.ncate.org

P.E.4LIFE is an advocacy group that promotes more and better physical education in schools. For more information, contact
P.E.4LIFE
http://www.pe4life.org

For comprehensive resources for health and physical educators, visit
PE Central
http://www.pecentral.org

INTERVIEW

Philip Lawler has been the district coordinator of physical education for Naperville Community Unit School District 203 (IL) for 17 years. The District has two high schools, five junior high schools, and 14 elementary schools, and has an enrollment of approximately 18,000 students. Mr. Lawler also teaches at Madison Junior High School, one of the schools in his District. Madison is an excellent example of how the New PE, now often called P.E.4LIFE, is changing the lives of young people. Mr. Lawler spoke with the editors of Careers in Focus: Coaches & Fitness Professionals *about his district's physical education program and the career of physical education teacher.*

Q. How would you define P.E.4LIFE?

A. P.E.4LIFE is a model that creates healthy habits for children that will last a lifetime.

Q. Please describe the physical education (PE) program at Madison Junior High School. How is it different from PE programs of the past?

A. Our program is designed to meet the needs of every child. The sports model used for years only met the needs of a small percentage of our students. Our program focuses on health, wellness, and lifestyle management.

 We have a serious health care issue in our country, and quality daily physical education is the only long-term solution that makes sense. Educating adults to change lifestyle habits has not worked. We must begin with children and create good health habits.

Q. What kind of results have you seen with your program? How have your students responded?

A. In a survey, parents rated physical education as the number one curriculum for curriculum satisfaction. Parents rated physical education above science, math, and English. Considering that our program focuses on the health of children, the rating did not surprise us.

 We tested 1,500 freshmen over two years, and 97 percent of these students were in the healthy zone in body composition. During this epidemic of obesity [in our nation's children], the nation should look at the amazing results of our program.

Q. What personal qualities does a physical education teacher need to be successful in this field?

A. Young teachers must have a vision. They must understand the value of quality physical education. They must ask themselves the important question "what do I want a student to know and be able to do because they have been in my class." Children must be lifelong learners. We must look at the delivery of physical education and ask ourselves "what am I teaching that will be important to the child, not just now, but when they are an adult?"

Q. What advice would you give to an aspiring physical education teacher?

A. There has never been a better time for a career in physical education. For years, physical education teachers were never respected, but the public is beginning to value quality physical education. A doctor recently visited our program, and he made an interesting comment at the end of his visit. He said "if physical education was taught around the nation as it is delivered in Madison Junior High School, PE teachers can do more to affect the health of our nation than I can as a doctor." This was a very powerful message.

I would also recommend that all aspiring physical education teachers visit the P.E.4LIFE website, http://www.pe4life.org. P.E.4LIFE is helping lead the charge by educating the nation about the importance of quality daily physical education in our schools.

Professional Sports Coaches

OVERVIEW

Professional sports coaches instruct and manage professional athletes. These athletes compete in individual-player sports such as tennis, figure skating, golf, track and field, and boxing, or as members of baseball, football, basketball, hockey, soccer, and other sports teams. Coaches prepare their players for competition. During competition, coaches oversee their players and use their knowledge of the sport to try to beat the opposing player or team. Over 90,000 elementary, secondary, postsecondary, and professional sports coaches are employed in the United States. Professional coaches comprise a very small percentage of this group.

HISTORY

Prior to the 19th century, most sports were not officially organized; there were no official rules, competitions, or standards of play. During the 19th century, however, many sports shifted from invented pastime to official sport. Rules governing play, the field of play, and the nature of competitions were developed. The first modern track-and-field meet, for example, was held in England in 1825. Meanwhile, in the United States, the English game of rugby evolved into American football. The first game was played between Rutgers University and Princeton University in 1869. Baseball was invented in 1839, and the first professional league was formed in 1876. The game of basketball was invented in 1891 by James Naismith, a young physical education teacher in Springfield, Massachusetts.

Baseball, basketball, golf, tennis, and boxing began to attract large crowds of people in the early 20th century. As these sports and others grew in popularity, governing bodies and organizations were created to oversee the fair play of each sport. Gradually, coverage of sporting events in newspapers and on the radio began to grow until sports quite literally became the national pastime for Americans. As sports grew in popularity and professional leagues were formed for all the major sports, professional coaches were increasingly relied on to manage and teach players.

Today, professional sports are still growing in popularity, and professional coaches enjoy considerable prestige and high salaries. Coaches may not be as popular as star athletes, but they still play a very important role in sports competition.

THE JOB

Many professional teams have several coaches per team. *Head coaches* are the top coaches of a sports team. They are assisted by *assistant coaches,* who specialize in one aspect of the sport. In professional baseball, for example, the head coach, known as a *manager,* oversees a group of coaches with specialized skills. These assistant coaches include a *bench coach,* who assists the manager in game situations; a *pitching coach,* who works with the team's starting and relief pitchers; a *hitting* or *batting coach,* who works with the team's hitters; a *bullpen coach,* who is responsible for making sure that pitchers warm up correctly before they enter a game; *first* and *third base coaches,* who advise players on base-running after they reach base; and *strength and conditioning coaches,* who help players maintain top performance levels. Some Major League Baseball teams may even have a coach who teaches players proper base-running techniques.

Coaches oversee practices and workouts to help athletes develop fundamental skills and condition their bodies for competition. They use lectures and demonstrations to instruct their players on the proper way to play their sports. Professional sports coaches are experts in the rules and strategies for their respective sports. They use this expertise to make decisions during games. Coaches are also responsible for maintaining team discipline. Professional athletes occasionally behave poorly on and off the field. Coaches must address these behavioral problems or other issues that may affect the team's performance. Coaches must be consistent and fair when assessing penalties for misbehavior, otherwise they will lose the confidence of their team.

Professional athletes are the top athletes in their sports. It is assumed, but not always true, that they are experts at every aspect of their sport, from blocking and running offensive routes in football to fielding a ground ball and bunting in baseball. If a player is deficient in an area, a sports coach may work with the player to improve his or her abilities or assign an assistant coach to help the player.

Most coaches will tell you that psychological preparation is every bit as important as physical training in professional-level sports. One of the most important and challenging jobs for a professional coach is the motivation of star athletes who sometimes do not give maximum effort during competition. It is the coach's job to motivate athletes to give their best effort in every game as well as make sacrifices for the benefit of the team. Players require different motivation methods based on their personalities. Some players respond well to criticism, while others may respond better to positive reinforcement. Coaches must know what psychological approach to use with each player.

All professional sports leagues have a preseason when teams compete in exhibition games. Sports coaches use this exhibition season to teach players fundamental skills, help players regain top levels of conditioning lost during the offseason, and evaluate new and current players to determine if they have the ability to be part of the team. By the end of the preseason, the coach must choose a final group of players that will make up the team. The remaining players are released (the equivalent of being fired from a traditional job) or sent to the minor or lower level leagues for more training and experience. Sports coaches must explain to these players why they did not make the team and give them encouragement and tips on how to eventually make it to the professional level.

To prepare for competition, coaches develop game plans based on the skills and talents of their athletes and the strengths and weaknesses of the opposing team or athlete. They go over these game plans with their players, covering any scenarios that may occur during competition. In team sports such as basketball, soccer, and baseball, coaches choose a starting lineup and have a general idea of which players they will substitute into the game. Game action also affects how a coach uses his or her players. For example, an injury to a player early in a game might force the coach to alter his or her game plan.

During competition, professional coaches analyze their team's play and revise their strategy if necessary. They substitute players into the game if a starting player gets tired, is injured, or is not performing up to his or her abilities. They also substitute players for strategic reasons. (In the team sport of baseball, a player cannot reenter the game after he is removed by the manager. For this reason, baseball managers need strong organizational skills to keep track of which players have been used and which players are still available for competition.) Coaches need to keep track of timeouts, playing time remaining in the game, the number of fouls each player has received, and other issues.

On off days, coaches review videotape of recent games to assess the performances of their players. They take notes on the tendencies and actions of the opposing team's players to plan for future contests between the teams. Coaches meet with assistant coaches to discuss player issues or develop strategy for upcoming games.

Coaches work with general managers and other top management to assess players. They offer advice on which players the team should acquire through amateur drafts or through trades or free agent signings. Sports coaches also work with sports nutritionists, team physicians, sports trainers, sports psychologists, exercise psychologists, sports scouts, and marketing and public relations specialists.

Sports coaches also have administrative responsibilities. They attend league meetings with owners, assistant coaches, and *general managers,* who oversee the day-to-day operations of the team. Coaches hire and fire assistant coaches. If a coaching vacancy occurs, coaches interview candidates and choose a replacement. In some sports, the general manager may be responsible for hiring and firing coaches.

Coaches meet with newspaper, radio, and television reporters before and after games to discuss their players and the decisions they made during a game. Coaches also speak at charity events, awards dinners, and fan fests, and on radio and television talk shows.

REQUIREMENTS

High School
To prepare for a coaching career, you should take physical education, human physiology, biology, psychology, and health classes. Courses in English and speech will help you to communicate effectively with your players, assistant coaches, and team management. Participation in high school sports will give you useful exposure to competition, rules and regulations, and game situations—skills you will need as a coach.

Postsecondary Training
A college degree is not required to become a professional sports coach, but many coaches often attended college as athletes. Since no one begins their coaching career at the professional level, it is vital that you earn a college degree so that you will have a firm educational

background as you work your way up the coaching ladder. Many coaches earn degrees in business, recreation, education, sports management, or other subject areas in which they have an interest. Aspiring coaches often begin their coaching careers at the high school and college levels. Most high school and college coaches work as teachers in addition to their coaching duties. To become a teacher, you will need at least a bachelor's degree in education, physical education, or another area of interest.

Other Requirements

To be a successful professional coach, you must have an encyclopedic knowledge of the sport that you coach. You also need to have considerable playing and coaching experience. You should be a good communicator in order to instruct and interact successfully with your players and assistant coaches, team management, and the media. You also need to be disciplined and have the patience to accept mistakes and losses. Coaches must also be able to work in high-pressure situations and be able to accept criticism from fans and media during losing streaks.

You will also need to stay up to date with new coaching techniques and rule procedures, have a desire to continue to learn, and be willing to try new strategies and techniques.

EXPLORING

Begin coaching and playing sports as early as possible. Get involved in school or community leagues in a variety of sports. Attend sporting events as a spectator. Observe how the head coach manages and interacts with players, and think about what you would do in various game situations. If you are a member of a team, talk with your sports coach about his or her career, or ask your school guidance counselor to set up an informational interview with a sports coach in your community.

EMPLOYERS

Professional sports coaches are employed by private and public ownership groups all over the world. At the highest professional level for male athletes, there are 32 National Football League franchises, 30 Major League Baseball franchises, 29 National Basketball Association franchises, 30 National Hockey League franchises, and 10 Major League Soccer franchises in the United States and Canada. The Women's National Basketball Association has 14 franchises in the United States. Most professional sports leagues also have minor leagues that employ sports coaches. Professional sports coaches who coach individual players in tennis, figure skating, and other individual sports are usually self-employed.

STARTING OUT

Professional sports coaching is not an entry-level career. Almost every professional sports coach played and coached for many years in high school, college, or the minor leagues before being hired at the professional level. Once you establish a proven track record as a coach, you will be able to pursue more lucrative and challenging coaching positions at higher professional levels.

If you are interested in coaching at the college level, you might try to land a job as a *graduate assistant coach*. Graduate assistant coaches are recently graduated players who are interested in becoming coaches. You will receive a small stipend and, more importantly, gain valuable coaching experience.

ADVANCEMENT

Professional sports coaches advance based on their individual skills and coaching abilities. Assistant coaches can advance to fill head coaching positions with their team or another team. Some head coaches advance to the position of general manager. Occasionally, a top coach may work as both head coach and general manager. Coaches of individual-player sports advance by coaching athletes who consistently win competitions. This allows them to ask for higher salaries and be more selective regarding clients and work schedules.

EARNINGS

Salaries for professional sports coaches vary widely depending on the sport, the person or team being coached, and the skill level of the coach. The coach of a Masters champion, for example, commands a higher salary than the coach of a professional golf player who has never won a tournament. The coach of a Super Bowl champion earns a lot more than a rookie coach who has no proven track record in the National Football League.

The U.S. Department of Labor reports that the median earnings for sports coaches at all levels of competition were $29,030 in 2001. The lowest paid 10 percent earned less than $13,410, while the highest paid 10 percent earned more than $62,560.

New York Yankees manager Joe Torre signals for a pitching change. (*Corbis*)

Coaches for professional teams often earn between $200,000 and $3 million. Some top coaches command even higher salaries. The highest paid coaches in the National Basketball Association earn between $6 million and $7 million annually. Top coaches in Major League Baseball earn between $5 million and $6 million annually, while the highest paid National Football League coaches earn $5 million a year. Professional sports coaches usually receive two- to five-year contracts based on their past experience as head or assistant coaches on winning teams. Many popular coaches augment their salaries with income from personal appearances and endorsements.

WORK ENVIRONMENT

The work environment for professional sports coaches varies by sport. Many professional sports competitions such as football, baseball, soccer, and track are held both indoors and outdoors. Other sports, such as basketball and hockey, take place only indoors. Indoor competitions are held in climate-controlled stadiums. Outdoor competitions take place in a variety of weather conditions depending on the sport. For example, a professional football team may play one game in wintry conditions in Wisconsin and their next game in warm and sunny Florida.

Professional sports teams compete all over the world. They play exhibition or real games in other countries. Professional coaches and athletes usually travel by plane, but occasionally they travel to nearby cities by bus or train. They usually stay in first-class hotels when traveling.

Coaches often work 16 hours each day, five or six days a week during their playing season. They often spend their off days analyzing game film or making public appearances. Many games are held on nights and weekends because this is when fans are able to watch teams play. This busy schedule can be tough on a coach's personal life.

There is little job security in professional sports coaching. Professional sports is big business, and sports media, fans, and team owners expect professional sports coaches to produce winning teams. When their teams don't perform up to expectations, coaches are often fired or reassigned. Coaches can be fired at any time, but they still receive their salaries if they are under contract.

OUTLOOK

Professional sports leagues employ relatively few coaches, and competition for existing jobs is very strong. The creation of new professional leagues, as well as the expansion of current leagues, will open some new employment opportunities for professional coaches. Other openings will arise as coaches retire or are terminated. Coaching is an exciting, demanding profession, but there is little job security in this field.

FOR MORE INFORMATION

For general information on sports and fitness, contact
American Alliance for Health, Physical Education, Recreation and Dance
1900 Association Drive
Reston, VA 20191-1598
Tel: 800-213-7193
http://www.aahperd.org

For information on careers in sports and physical education, contact
National Association for Sport and Physical Education
1900 Association Drive
Reston, VA 20191-1598
Tel: 800-213-7193
Email: naspe@aahperd.org
http://www.aahperd.org/naspe

Visit the following websites for more information on professional sports:

Association of Tennis Professionals
http://www.atptennis.com

Ladies Professional Golf Association
http://www.lpga.com

Major League Baseball
http://www.mlb.com

Major League Soccer
http://www.mlsnet.com

National Basketball Association
http://www.nba.com

National Football League
http://nfl.com

National Hockey League
http://www.nhl.com

Professional Golf Association
http://www.pga.com

Women's National Basketball Association
http://www.wnba.com

Visit the Coaches Corner *section of the following website for tennis coaching tips and profiles of coaches:*

Women's Tennis Association
http://www.wtatour.com

Recreational Therapists

OVERVIEW

Recreational therapists plan, organize, direct, and monitor medically approved recreation programs for patients in hospitals, clinics, and various community settings. These therapists use recreational activities to assist patients with mental, physical, or emotional disabilities to achieve the maximum possible functional independence. Recreational therapists hold almost 27,000 jobs in the United States.

HISTORY

The field of therapy has expanded in the past few decades to include recreational therapy as a form of medical treatment. Its use grew out of the realization that soldiers suffering from battle fatigue, shock, and emotional trauma respond positively to organized recreation and activity programs.

As a result, people in nursing homes, hospitals, mental institutions, and adult-care facilities are no longer limited to physical therapy. Experiments have shown that recovery is aided by recreational activities such as sports, music, art, gardening, dance, drama, field trips, and other pastimes. Elderly people are more healthy and alert when their days are filled with activities, field trips, and social get-togethers. People with disabilities can gain greater self-confidence and awareness of their own abilities when they get involved with sports, crafts, and other activities. People recovering from drug or alcohol addiction can reaffirm their self-worth through directed, enjoyable hobbies, clubs, and sports. The recreational therapist is a health professional who organizes these types of activities and helps patients take an active role in their own recovery.

THE JOB

Recreational therapists work with people who are mentally, physically, or emotionally disabled. They are professionals who employ leisure activities as a form of treatment, much as other health practitioners use surgery, drugs, nutrition, exercise, or psychotherapy. Recreational therapists strive to minimize patients' symptoms, restore function, and improve their physical, mental, and emotional well being. Enhancing the patient's ability to take part in everyday life is the primary goal of recreational therapy; interesting and rewarding activities are the means for working toward that goal.

Recreational therapists work in a number of different settings, including mental hospitals, psychiatric day hospitals, community mental health centers, nursing homes, adult day care programs, residential facilities for the mentally disabled, school systems, and prisons. They can work as individual staff members, as independent consultants, or as part of a larger therapeutic team. They may get personally involved with patients or direct the work of assistants and support staff.

The recreational therapist first confers with the doctors, psychiatrists, social workers, physical therapists, and other professionals on staff to coordinate their efforts in treatment. The recreational therapist needs to understand the nature of the patient's ailment, current physical and mental capacities, emotional state, and prospects for recovery. The patient's family and friends are also consulted to find out the patient's interests and hobbies. With this information, the recreational therapist then plans an agenda of activities for that person.

To enrich the lives of people in hospitals and other institutions, recreational therapists use imagination and skill in organizing beneficial activities. Sports, games, arts and crafts, movie screenings, field trips, hobby clubs, and dramatics are only a few examples of activities that can enrich the lives of patients. Some therapists specialize in certain areas. *Dance/movement therapists* plan and conduct dance and body movement exercises to improve patients' physical and mental well being. *Art therapists* work with patients in various art methods, such as drawing, painting, and ceramics, as part of their therapeutic and recovery programs. Therapists may also work with pets and other animals, such as horses. *Music therapists* design programs for patients that can involve solo or group singing, playing in bands, rhythmic and other creative activities, listening to music, or attending concerts. Even flowers and gardening can prove beneficial to patients, as is proved by the work of *horticultural therapists*. When the treatment team feels that regular employment would help certain patients, the *industrial therapist* arranges a productive job for the patient in an actual work environment, one that will have the greatest therapeutic value based on the patient's needs and abilities. *Orientation therapists* for the blind work with people who have recently lost their sight, helping them to readjust to daily living and independence through training and exercise. All of these professional therapists plan their programs to meet the needs and capabilities of patients. They also carefully monitor and record each patient's progress and report it to the other members of the medical team.

As part of their jobs, recreational therapists need to understand their patients and set goals for their progress accordingly. A patient having trouble socializing, for example, may have an interest in playing chess but be overwhelmed by the prospect of actually playing, since that involves interaction with another person. A therapist would proceed slowly, first letting the patient observe a number of games and then assigning a therapeutic assistant to serve as a chess partner for as long as it takes for the patient to gain enough confidence to seek out other patients for chess partners. The therapist makes a note of the patient's response, modifies the therapy program accordingly, and lets other professionals know of the results. If a patient responds more enthusiastically to the program, works more cooperatively with others, or becomes more disruptive, the therapist must note these reactions and periodically reevaluate the patient's activity program.

Responsibilities and elements of the job can vary, depending on the setting in which the recreational therapist works. In nursing homes, the therapist often groups residents according to common or shared interests and ability levels and then plans field trips, parties, entertainment, and other group activities. The therapist documents residents' responses to the activities and continually searches for ways of heightening residents' enjoyment of recreational and leisure activities, not just in the facility but in the surrounding community as well. Because nursing home residents are likely to remain in the facility for months or even years, the activities program makes a big difference in the quality of their lives. Without the stimulation of interesting events to look forward to and participate in, the daily routine of a nursing home can become monotonous and depressing, and some residents are apt to deteriorate both mentally and physically. In some nursing homes, recreational therapists direct the activities program. In others, *activities coordinators* plan and carry out the program under the part-time supervision of a consultant who is either a recreational or occupational therapist.

The therapist in a community center might work in a day-care program for the elderly or in a program for mentally disabled adults operated by a county recreation department. No matter what the disability, recreational therapists in community settings face the added logistical challenge of arranging transportation and escort services, if necessary, for prospective participants. Coordinating transportation is less of a problem in hospitals and nursing homes, where the patients all live under one roof. Developing therapeutic recreation programs in community settings requires a large measure of organizational ability, flexibility, and ingenuity.

Recreational therapy is a relatively new field, but it is already a respected, integral part of the treatment of many elderly and disabled people. Clients often need extra encouragement and support to stay active and build on the things they can, rather than can't, do. The activity programs that recreational therapists design and operate can add immeasurable enjoyment to the lives of patients. Beyond this, the activities provide opportunities for exercise and social interaction and may also help relieve anxiety and loneliness, build confidence, and promote each patient's independence.

REQUIREMENTS

High School
You can prepare for a career as a recreational therapist by taking your high school's college preparatory program. Naturally, this should include science classes, such as biology and chemistry, as well as mathematics and history classes. You can begin to gain an understanding of human behavior by taking psychology and sociology classes. For exposure to a variety of recreation specialties, take physical education, art, music, and drama classes. Verbal and written communication skills are essential for this work, so take English and speech classes. This job will require you to write reports, so computer science skills are also essential.

Postsecondary Training
Approximately 150 recreational therapy programs, which offer degrees ranging from the associate to the doctoral level, are currently available in the United States. While associate degrees in recreational therapy exist, such a degree will allow you only to work

at the paraprofessional level. To be eligible for an entry-level professional position as a recreational therapist, you will need a bachelor's degree. Acceptable majors are recreational therapy, therapeutic recreation, and recreation with a concentration in therapeutic recreation. A typical four-year bachelor's degree program includes courses in both natural science (such as biology, behavioral science, and human anatomy) and social science (such as psychology and sociology). Courses more specific to the profession include programming for special populations; rehabilitative techniques including self-help skills, mobility, signing for the deaf, and orientation for the blind; medical equipment; current treatment approaches; legal issues; and professional ethics. In addition, you will need to complete a supervised internship or field placement lasting a minimum of 480 hours.

Continuing education is increasingly becoming a requirement for professionals in this field. Many therapists attend conferences and seminars and take additional university courses. A number of professional organizations (for example, the National Therapeutic Recreation Society, the American Therapeutic Recreation Association, and the American Alliance for Health, Physical Education, Recreation, and Dance) offer continuing education opportunities. Those with degrees in related fields can enter the profession by earning master's degrees in therapeutic recreation. Advanced degrees are recommended for those seeking advancement to supervisory, administrative, and teaching positions. These requirements will become more strict as more professionals enter the field.

Certification or Licensing

A number of states regulate the profession of therapeutic recreation. Licensing is required in some states; professional certification (or eligibility for certification) is required in others; titling is regulated in some states and at some facilities. In other states, many hospitals and other employers require recreational therapists to be certified. Certification is recommended for recreational therapists as a way to show professional accomplishment. It is available through the National Council for Therapeutic Recreation Certification. To receive certification you must meet eligibility requirements, including education and experience, as well as pass an exam. You are then given the title certified therapeutic recreation specialist (CTRS). Because of the variety of certification and licensing requirements, you must check with both your state and your employer for specific information on your situation.

Other Requirements

To be a successful recreational therapist, you must, of course, enjoy and be enthusiastic about the activities in which you involve your clients. You will also need patience and a positive attitude. Since this is people-oriented work, therapists must be able to relate to many different people in a variety of settings. They must be able to deal assertively and politely with other health care workers, such as doctors and nurses, as well as with the clients themselves and their families. In addition, successful therapists must be creative and have strong communication skills in order to develop and explain activities to patients.

EXPLORING

If you are interested in recreational therapy, you can find part-time or summer work as a sports coach or referee, park supervisor, or camp counselor. Volunteer work in a nursing home, hospital, or care facility for disabled adults is also a good way to learn about the daily realities of institutional living. These types of facilities are always looking for volunteers to work with and visit patients. Working with people with physical, mental, or emotional disabilities can be stressful, and volunteer work is a good way for you to test whether you can handle this kind of stress.

EMPLOYERS

Recreational therapists hold almost 27,000 jobs, according to the U.S. Department of Labor. Almost 40 percent of these jobs are in nursing and personal care facilities, and more than 30 percent are in hospitals. Other employers include residential facilities, adult day care centers, and substance abuse centers, and some therapists are self-employed. Employment opportunities also exist in long-term rehabilitation, home health care, correctional facilities, psychiatric facilities, and transitional programs.

STARTING OUT

There are many methods for finding out about available jobs in recreational therapy. A good place to start is the job notices and want ads printed in the local newspapers, bulletins from state park and recreation societies, and publications of the professional associations previously mentioned. State employment agencies and human service departments will know of job openings in state hospitals. College placement offices might also be able to put new recreational therapy graduates in touch with prospective employers. Internship programs are sometimes available, offering good opportunities to find potential full-time jobs.

Recent graduates should also make appointments to meet potential employers personally. Most colleges and universities offer career counseling services. Most employers will make themselves available to discuss their programs and the possibility of hiring extra staff. They may also guide new graduates to other institutions currently hiring therapists. Joining professional associations, both state and national, and attending conferences are good ways to meet potential employers and colleagues.

ADVANCEMENT

Newly graduated recreational therapists generally begin as staff therapists. Advancement is chiefly to supervisory or administrative positions, usually after some years of experience and continuing education. Some therapists teach, conduct research, or do consulting work on a contract basis; a graduate degree is essential for moving into these areas.

Many therapists continue their education but prefer to continue working with patients. For variety, they may choose to work with new groups of people or get a job in a new setting, such as moving from a retirement home to a facility for the disabled. Some may also move to a related field, such as special education, or sales positions involving products and services related to recreational therapy.

EARNINGS

Salaries of recreational therapists vary according to educational background, experience, certification, and region of the country. Recreational therapists had median earnings of $30,030 in 2001, according to the U.S. Department of Labor. The lowest paid 10 percent earned less than $17,940 a year, while the highest paid 10 percent earned more than $45,960 annually. Employment setting is also an important factor in determining salary. For example, the *Occupational Outlook Handbook* reported that recreational therapists employed by hospitals had median incomes of $32,520 in 2000, while those working for personal care agencies and nursing facilities earned median incomes of $23,240. Those in management positions command higher salaries. Supervisors reported top salaries of $50,000 per year; administrators reported maximum earnings of

$65,000 annually; and some consultants and educators reported even higher earnings.

Therapists employed at hospitals, clinics, and other facilities generally enjoy a full benefit package, including health insurance and vacation, holiday, and sick pay. Consultants and self-employed therapists must provide their own benefits.

WORK ENVIRONMENT

Working conditions vary, but recreational therapists generally work in a ward, a specially equipped activity room, or at a nursing home. In a community setting, recreational therapists may interview subjects and plan activities in an office, but they might work in a gymnasium, swimming pool, playground, or outdoors on a nature walk when leading activities. Therapists may also work on horse ranches, farms, and other outdoor facilities catering to people with disabilities.

The job may be physically tiring because therapists are often on their feet all day and may have to lift and carry equipment. Recreational therapists generally work a standard 40-hour week, although weekend and evening hours may be required. Supervisors may have to work overtime, depending on their workload.

OUTLOOK

The U.S. Department of Labor predicts that employment for recreational therapists will grow more slowly than the average over the next several years. Employment will decline slightly in hospitals and nursing homes, which are expected to shift recreational therapy services to outpatient settings. Fast employment growth is expected in assisted living, outpatient physical and psychiatric rehabilitation, and services for people with disabilities. Increased life expectancies of the elderly and people with developmental disabilities such as Down's Syndrome will create opportunities for recreational therapists. The incidence of alcohol and drug dependency problems is also growing, creating a demand for qualified therapists to work in short-term alcohol and drug abuse clinics.

Most openings for recreational therapists will be in health care and assisted living facilities because of the increasing numbers and greater longevity of the elderly. There is also greater public pressure to regulate and improve the quality of life in retirement centers, which may mean more jobs and increased scrutiny of recreational therapists.

Growth in hospital jobs is not expected to be great. Many of the new jobs created will be in hospital-based adult day care programs or in units offering short-term mental health services. Because of economic and social factors, no growth is expected in public mental hospitals. Many of the programs and services formerly offered there are being shifted to community residential facilities for the disabled. Community programs for special populations are expected to expand significantly.

FOR MORE INFORMATION

For career information and resources, contact
American Association for Leisure and Recreation
1900 Association Drive
Reston, VA 20191
Tel: 703-476-6527
Email: aalr@aahperd.org
http://www.aahperd.org/aalr

For career information, a list of colleges and universities that offer training, and job listings, contact
American Therapeutic Recreation Association
1414 Prince Street, Suite 204
Alexandria, VA 22314
Tel: 703-683-9420
Email: atra@atra-tr.org
http://www.atra-tr.org

For information on certification, contact
National Council for Therapeutic Recreation Certification
7 Elmwood Drive
New City, NY 10956
Tel: 845-639-1439
Email: nctrc@nctrc.org
http://www.nctrc.org

For career information, visit the NTRS under Branches *on the website of the National Recreation and Park Association.*
National Therapeutic Recreation Society (NTRS)
22377 Belmont Ridge Road
Ashburn, VA 20148
Tel: 703-858-0784
Email: ntrsnrpa@nrpa.org
http://www.nrpa.org

Visit this website to find out about jobs, activities, schools, and other information related to the field.
Therapeutic Recreation Directory
http://www.recreationtherapy.com

─────────────── **INTERVIEW** ───────────────

Dana R. Dempsey is the director of therapeutic recreation (TR) and child life at Texas Scottish Rite Hospital for Children in Dallas, Texas. She spoke with the editors of Careers in Focus: Coaches & Fitness Professionals *about her career and the field of recreational therapy.*

Q. What are your primary and secondary job duties as a recreational therapist?

A. My primary job is to help people who have a medical condition or disability learn the skills they need to be as independent as possible in recreation and leisure activities. My secondary job is to help educate people within the community at large about the importance of making recreation and leisure opportunities available to individuals who have disabilities.

Q. Please describe your work setting.

A. My work setting is very unique. I work at Texas Scottish Rite Hospital for Children. It is a pediatric orthopedic hospital that provides medical care for children from birth to age 18 who live in the state of Texas and who have a wide range of orthopedic disabilities, neurological disorders, and learning differences. Families are never billed for any of the medical care, including the therapeutic recreation services. Our hospital operates off of donations from organizations and individuals. This is important because it allows us to focus on what is best for the child without having to be limited by what insurance will cover. This has given us the opportunity to develop therapeutic recreation programs that cross setting boundaries. Our hospital has three primary focuses: medical care, research, and teaching. Because of our unique setting, I travel regularly for my job. My travel has been to work with our patients around the state of Texas, and I've been fortunate to speak at conferences around the United States and in Mexico about therapeutic recreation.

Q. How did you train for this career?

A. I received both a bachelor of science and master of science degree in therapeutic recreation from the University of North Texas. As an undergraduate student I minored in psychology, and as a graduate student my minor was business. As a part of my B.S. degree program, I was required to complete an internship under the supervision of a certified therapeutic recreation specialist (CTRS). Upon completion of my degree and internship, I was eligible to sit for the national exam given by the National Council for Therapeutic Recreation Certification (NCTRC). Fortunately, I passed the exam and now have the credential of CTRS. While school and the training needed to sit for the exam provided an excellent foundation, much of what has prepared me to do the job at Scottish Rite has been my experiences working in this field. I have been very fortunate to have outstanding mentors along the way.

Q. Did this major in therapeutic recreation prepare you for your career or, in retrospect, would you pursue another major? If so, what major?

A. I do feel that my major prepared me for my career. TR is a profession of serving others. TR provides the opportunity to work in a wide variety of settings. I feel strongly that one is only limited by their creativity in how they might use their knowledge and skills to help individuals' with a disability reach their own potential within their leisure involvement. I love what I do! I have a passion for it and feel that I have received back as much if not more than what I have put into my profession.

Q. Where did you get your first job in the field?

A. I worked a variety of jobs while going to college; many of the jobs were in recreation and leisure settings (e.g., parks and recreation department, dude ranch, country club, children's home). However, my first job after graduation was at Terrell State Hospital. I was hired to provide therapeutic recreation programs for adult patients who had a dual diagnosis of mental illness and mental retardation. Since the patients with whom I worked all lived at the hospital, much of my job involved having the patients actively involved in recreational activities both on campus and in the community. Besides teaching activity skills, I taught a lot of leisure-related skills (i.e., social interaction, problem solving, leisure planning, anger management, etc.) to my patients so that they could be more self-directed in their recreation and more successful in community social settings. I also did a lot of support work when needed. For example, many of my patients had expressed a desire to have a garden but they were not physically able to do much of the soil prep work. Therefore, I tilled and weeded the garden area to prepare it so patients would be able to do the plantings and help with maintaining the garden.

Q. How can someone who is interested in the field of recreational therapy learn more?

A. There are many sources a person could turn to when looking to get into the TR field. I would first suggest contacting the American Therapeutic Recreation Association (http://www.atra-tr.org), which is the largest professional association for TR. Another resource would be the NCTRC (http://www.nctrc.org). Both of these organizations are happy to answer questions one might have about getting into the field of TR. They can also connect a person to a college or university that offer TR as a field of study. Other resources include the TR Directory (http://www. recreationtherapy.com) and the National Therapeutic Recreation Society (http://www.activeparks.org).

Q. What are the most important personal and professional qualities for recreational therapists?

A. Some of the important qualities for practitioners in my field include a strong desire to serve others, a desire to make a difference, patience, self-motivation, and a love of people. Professionally, it is important to have good planning, communication, interpersonal, and organizational skills. It is also important to understand that being in the profession also means giving back to the profession by being an active member of a professional association and serving in leadership roles (i.e., intern supervisor, committee, task force, board of directors, etc.).

Q. What are the best and worst parts of your job?

A. The biggest pro is that, at the end of the day, I feel really good about what I've done. I know without a doubt I made a difference—even if it was short lived. TR allows one to "play for a living." And while many job tasks are not that enjoyable, there are many tasks that are just downright fun! Regardless of the age of the individual I have worked with, I feel very humble and blessed to have seen the joy or sense of accomplishment the person experienced during their leisure. Another pro is that I get to work in leisure settings, wearing clothes that are appropriate for leisure activities. I find it neat that one day I may be in a business suit talking in front of a room full of business professionals, and the next day I'm wearing shorts, a pullover shirt, and sneakers teaching a child how to play bocce ball or ride a handcycle.

I think the cons in our profession revolve around lack of respect, recognition, and reimbursement. Too often, people do not understand therapeutic recreation or the role it can play in a person's life. We also live in a society that has very mixed messages about recreation and leisure. While most people can hardly wait for their "time off" or spend a great amount of time, money, and energy planning their next vacation, our society often devalues recreation, leisure, and play. Somehow, play loses its importance and one can even be made to feel guilty for "just playing around." It is easy to look around and see examples of how little value we place on recreation and leisure when parks and recreation programs are usually the first to be hit with budget cuts. Insurance companies will generally not pay for "sport" wheelchairs and many times it is a fight to have TR services reimbursed by third-party payers. Salaries of people within the TR field are generally lower than other allied health care professionals.

Q. What advice would you give to college students who plan to enter this field?

A. Love what you do, and use your education, training, and skills to utilize the TR process to provide programs and interventions for the people you are serving—regardless of your work setting.

Q. What is the future employment outlook for recreational therapists?

A. According to the U.S. Department of Labor's *Occupational Outlook Handbook,* the profession will "grow more slowly than average for all occupations through the year 2010." Regardless of whether that comes to pass, I do think that there will always be a need for certified therapeutic recreation specialists. I agree with the *Handbook* that we will see a shift from hospital and nursing home settings to a greater need in a variety of community settings. More and more people who have a disability are gaining their voices and demanding that recreation and leisure service professionals provide opportunities for their involvement as well. It will be important for professionals working in therapeutic recreation to establish partnerships to educate and train not only those with disabilities but also the community at large.

Sports Instructors and Coaches

QUICK FACTS

School Subjects
English
Physical education

Personal Skills
Communication/ideas
Helping/teaching

Work Environment
Indoors and outdoors
Primarily multiple locations

Minimum Education Level
Some postsecondary training

Salary Range
$13,410 to $29,030 to
$2,000,000+

Certification or Licensing
Required in certain positions

Outlook
About as fast as the average

DOT
153

GOE
12.01.01

NOC
5252

O*NET-SOC
27-2022.00

OVERVIEW

Sports instructors demonstrate and explain the skills and rules of particular sports, like golf or tennis, to individuals or groups. They help beginners learn basic stances, grips, movements, and techniques of a game. Sports instructors often help experienced athletes to sharpen their skills.

Coaches work with a single, organized team or individual, teaching the skills associated with that sport. A coach prepares her or his team for competition, and during the competition he or she continues to give instruction from a vantage point near the court or playing field.

HISTORY

Americans have more leisure time than ever and many have decided that they are going to put this time to good use by getting or staying in shape. This fitness boom, as well as a trend toward more sports competition, have created employment opportunities for many sports-related occupations.

Health clubs, community centers, parks and recreational facilities, and private business now employ sports instructors who teach everything from tennis and golf to scuba diving.

As high school and college sports become even more organized, there is a continuing need for coaches qualified to teach the intricate skills needed to excel in different sports.

THE JOB

The specific job requirements of sports instructors and coaches varies according to the type of sport and who they teach. For example, an instructor teaching advanced skiing at a resort in Utah will have different duties and responsibilities than an instructor teaching beginning swimming at a municipal pool. Nevertheless, all instructors and coaches are teachers. They must be very knowledgeable about rules and strategies for their respective sports, but without an effective teaching method that reinforces correct techniques and procedures, their students or players won't be able to share that valuable knowledge. Also, instructors and coaches need to be aware of and open to new procedures and techniques. Many attend clinics or seminars to learn more about their sport or even how to teach more effectively. Many are members of professional organizations that deal exclusively with their sport.

Safety is a primary concern for all coaches and instructors. Coaches and instructors make sure their students have the right equipment and know its correct use. A major component of safety is helping students feel comfortable and confident with their abilities. This entails teaching the proper stances, techniques, and movements of a game, instructing students on basic rules, and answering any questions.

While instructors may tutor students individually or in small groups, a coach works with all the members of a team. Both use lectures and demonstrations to show students the proper skills, and both point out the mistakes or deficiencies of individuals.

Motivation is another key element in sports instruction. Almost all sports require stamina, and most coaches will tell you that psychological preparation is every bit as important as physical training.

Coaches and instructors also have administrative responsibilities. College coaches actively recruit new players to join their team. Professional coaches attend team meetings with owners and general managers to determine which players they will draft the next season. Sports instructors at health and athletic clubs schedule classes, lessons, and contests.

REQUIREMENTS

Training and educational requirements vary, depending on the specific sport and the ability level of students being instructed. Most coaches who are associated with schools have bachelor's degrees.

Many middle and high school coaches are also teachers within the school. Most instructors need to combine several years of successful experience in a particular sport with some educational background, preferably in teaching. A college degree is becoming more important as part of an instructor's background.

High School

To prepare for college courses, high school students should take courses that teach human physiology. Biology, health, and exercise classes would all be helpful. Courses in English and speech are also important to improve or develop communication skills.

There is no substitute for developing expertise in a sport. If you can play the sport well and can explain to other people how they might play as well as you, you will most likely be able to get a job as a sports instructor. The most significant source of training for this occupation is gained while on the job.

Postsecondary Training

Postsecondary training in this field varies greatly. College and professional coaches often attended college as athletes, while others attended college and received their degrees without playing a sport. If you are interested in becoming a high school coach, you will need a college degree because you will most likely be teaching as well as coaching. At the high school level, coaches spend their days teaching everything from physical education to English to mathematics, and so the college courses these coaches take vary greatly. Coaches of some youth league sports may not need a postsecondary degree, but they must have a solid understanding of their sport and of injury prevention.

Certification or Licensing

Many facilities require sports instructors to be certified. Information on certification is available from any organization that deals with the specific sport in which one might be interested.

Since most high school coaches also work as teachers, people interested in this job should plan to obtain teacher certification in their state.

Other Requirements

Coaches have to be experts in their sport. They must have complete knowledge of the rules and strategies of the game, so that they can creatively design effective plays and techniques for their athletes. But the requirements for this job do not end here. Good coaches are able to communicate their extensive knowledge to the athletes in a way that not only instructs the athletes, but also inspires them to perform to their fullest potential. Therefore, coaches are also teachers.

"I think I'm good at my job because I love working with people and because I'm disciplined in everything I do," says Dawn Shannahan, former assistant girls' basketball and track coach at Leyden High School in Franklin Park, Illinois. Discipline is important for athletes, as they must practice plays and techniques over and over again. Coaches who cannot demonstrate and encourage this type of discipline will have difficulty helping their athletes improve. Shannahan adds, "I've seen coaches who are really knowledgeable about their sport but who aren't patient enough to allow for mistakes or for learning." Patience can make all the difference between an effective coach and one who is unsuccessful.

Similarly, Shannahan says, "A coach shouldn't be a pessimist. The team could be losing by a lot, but you have to stay optimistic and encourage the players."

EXPLORING

Try to gain as much experience as possible in all sports and a specific sport in particular. It is never too early to start. High school and college offer great opportunities to participate in sporting events either as a player, manager, trainer, or in intramural leagues.

Most communities have sports programs such as Little League baseball or track and field meets sponsored by the Recreation Commission. Get involved by volunteering as a coach, umpire, or starter.

Talking with sports instructors already working in the field is also a good way to discover specific job information and find out about career opportunities.

EMPLOYERS

Besides working in high schools, coaches are hired by colleges and universities, professional sports teams, individual athletes such as tennis players, and by youth leagues, summer camps, and recreation centers.

STARTING OUT

People with expertise in a particular sport and are interested in becoming an instructor should apply directly to the appropriate facility. Sometimes a facility will provide training.

For those interested in coaching, many colleges offer positions to *graduate assistant coaches*. Graduate assistant coaches are recently graduated players who are interested in becoming coaches. They receive a stipend and gain valuable coaching experience.

ADVANCEMENT

Advancement opportunities for both instructors and coaches depend on the individual's skills, willingness to learn, and work ethic. A sports instructor's success can be measured by caliber of play and number of students. Successful instructors may become well known enough to open their own schools or camps, write books, or produce how-to videos.

Some would argue that, for professional coaches, a high percentage of wins is the only criterion for success. However coaches in the scholastic ranks have other responsibilities and other factors that measure success. High school and college coaches must make sure their players are getting good grades, and middle school coaches can be successful if they produce a team that competes in a sportsman-like fashion regardless of whether they win or lose.

Successful coaches are often hired by larger schools. High school coaches may advance to become college coaches, and the most successful college coaches often are given the opportunity to coach professional teams. Former players sometimes land assistant or head coaching positions.

EARNINGS

Earnings for sports instructors vary considerably depending on the sport and the person or team being coached. For example, the coach of a Wimbledon champion commands much more money per hour than the swimming instructor at the municipal pool.

The U.S. Department of Labor reports that the median earnings for sports coaches and instructors were $29,030 in 2001. The lowest 10 percent earned less than $13,410, while the highest 10 percent earned more than $62,560. Sports instructors and coaches who worked at colleges and universities earned a median annual salary of $32,880 in 2000, while those employed by elementary and secondary schools earned $27,970.

Much of the work is part time, and part-time employees generally do not receive paid vacations, sick days, or health insurance. Instructors who teach group classes for beginners through park districts or at city recreation centers can expect to earn around $6 per hour. An hour-long individual lesson through a golf course or tennis club averages $75. Many times, coaches for children's teams work as volunteers.

Many sports instructors work in camps teaching swimming, archery, sailing and other activities. These instructors generally earn between $1,000 and $2,500, plus room and board, for a summer session.

Full-time fitness instructors at gyms or health clubs can expect to earn between $16,000 and $37,000 per year. Instructors with many years of experience and college degree have the highest earning potential.

Most coaches who work at the high school level or below also teach within the school district. Besides their teaching salary and coaching fee—either a flat rate or a percentage of their annual salary—school coaches receive a benefits package that includes paid vacations and health insurance.

College head football coaches generally earn an average of $75,000, although top coaches can earn as much as $2 million per year. Head coaches of men's college basketball teams average about $70,000 annually, while coaches of women's teams average considerable less at $42,000 a year. Many larger universities pay more. Coaches for professional teams often earn between $125,000 and $500,000. Some top coaches can command salaries in the millions. Many popular coaches augment their salaries with personal appearances and endorsements.

WORK ENVIRONMENT

An instructor or coach may work indoors, in a gym or health club, or outdoors, perhaps at a swimming pool. Much of the work is part time. Full-time sports instructors generally work between 35 and 40 hours per week. During the season when their teams compete, coaches can work 16 hours each day, five or six days each week.

It's not unusual for coaches or instructors to work evenings or weekends. Instructors work then because that is when their adult students are available for instruction. Coaches work nights and weekends because those are the times their teams compete.

One significant drawback to this job is the lack of job security. A club may hire a new instructor on very little notice, or may cancel a scheduled class for lack of interest. Athletic teams routinely fire coaches after losing seasons.

Sports instructors and coaches should enjoy working with a wide variety of people. They should be able to communicate clearly and possess good leadership skills to teach complex skills effectively. They can take pride in the knowledge that they have helped their students or their players reach new heights of achievement and training.

OUTLOOK

Americans' interest in health, physical fitness, and body image continues to send people to gyms and playing fields. This fitness boom has created strong employment opportunities for many people in sports-related occupations.

According to the U.S. Department of Labor, this occupation will grow about as fast as the average over the next several years. Job opportunities will be greatest in urban areas, where population is the most dense. Health clubs, adult education programs, and private industry will require competent, dedicated instructors. Those with the most training, education, and experience will have the best chance for employment.

Coaching jobs at the high school or amateur level will be plentiful as long as the public continues its quest for a healthier and more active lifestyle. The creation of new professional leagues, as well as the expansion of current leagues, will open some new employment opportunities for professional coaches, but competition for these jobs will be very intense. There will also be openings as other coaches retire, or are terminated. However, there is very little job security in coaching, unless a coach can consistently produce a winning team.

FOR MORE INFORMATION

For certification information, trade journals, job listings, and a list of graduate schools, visit the AAHPERD website.

American Alliance for Health, Physical Education, Recreation and Dance (AAHPERD)
1900 Association Drive
Reston, VA 20191-1598
Tel: 800-213-7193
http://www.aahperd.org

For information on membership and baseball coaching education, coaching Web links, and job listings, visit the ABCA website.

American Baseball Coaches Association (ABCA)
108 South University Avenue, Suite 3
Mount Pleasant, MI 48858-2327
Tel: 989-775-3300

Email: abca@abca.org
http://www.abca.org

For information on careers in sports and physical education, contact
National Association for Sport and Physical Education
1900 Association Drive
Reston, VA 20191-1598
Tel: 800-213-7193
Email: naspe@aahperd.org
http://www.aahperd.org/naspe

For information on high school coaching opportunities, contact
National High School Athletic Coaches Association
PO Box 4342
Hamden, CT 06514
Tel: 203-288-7473
Email: office@hscoaches.org
http://www.hscoaches.org

Sports Physicians

QUICK FACTS

School Subjects
Biology
Health

Personal Skills
Helping/teaching

Work Environment
Indoors and outdoors
One location with some
  travel

Minimum Education Level
Medical degree

Salary Range
$46,700 to $118,400 to
  $1,000,000

Certification or Licensing
Required by all states

Outlook
About as fast as the average

DOT
070

GOE
02.03.01

NOC
3111

O*NET-SOC
29-1062.00, 29-1069.99

OVERVIEW

Sports physicians treat patients who have sustained injuries to their musculoskeletal systems during the play or practice of an individual or team sporting event. Sports physicians also do pre-participation tests and physical exams. Some sports physicians create educational programs to help athletes prevent injury. Sports physicians work for schools, universities, hospitals, and private offices; some also travel and treat members of professional sports teams.

HISTORY

The field of sports medicine, and nearly all the careers related to it, owes its foundation to the experiments and studies conducted by Aristotle, Leonardo da Vinci, and Etienne Jules Marey. Aristotle's treatise on the gaits of humans and animals established the beginning of biomechanics. In one experiment, he used the sun as a transducer to illustrate how a person, when walking in a straight line, actually throws a shadow that produces not a correspondingly straight line, but a zigzag line. Leonardo da Vinci's forays into the range and type of human motion explored a number of questions, including grade locomotion, wind resistance on the body, the projection of the center of gravity onto a base of support, and stepping and standing studies.

It was Marey, however, a French physiologist, who created much more advanced devices to study human motion. In fact, sports medicine and modern cinematography claim him as the father of their respective fields. Marey built the first force platform, a device which was able to visualize the forces between the foot and the

142

floor. His nonphotographic studies of the gait of a horse inspired Eadward Muybridge's serial photographs of a horse in motion, which in turn inspired Marey's invention of the chronophotograph. In contrast to Muybridge's consecutive frames, taken by several cameras, Marey's pictures with the chronophotograph superimposed the stages of action onto a single photograph; in essence, giving form to motion. By 1892, Marey had made primitive motion pictures, but his efforts were quickly eclipsed by those of Louis and Auguste Lumiere.

Following both World War I and II, Marey's and others scientists' experiments with motion would combine with medicine's need to heal and/or completely replace the limbs of war veterans. To provide an amputee with a prosthetic device that would come as close as possible to replicating the movement and functional value of a real limb, scientists and doctors began to work together at understanding the range of motion peculiar to the human body.

Mechanically, sports can be categorized according to the kinds of movements used. Each individual sport uses a unique combination of basic motions, including walking, running, jumping, kicking, and throwing. These basic motions have all been rigidly defined for scientific study so that injuries related to these motions can be better understood and treated. For example, sports that place heavy demands on one part of an athlete's body may overload that part and produce an injury, such as "tennis elbow" and "swimmer's shoulder." Baseball, on the other hand, is a throwing sport and certain injuries from overuse of the shoulder and elbow are expected. Athletes who play volleyball or golf also use some variation of the throwing motion and therefore, also sustain injuries to their shoulders and elbows.

Today, sports medicine in particular deals with the treatment and prevention of injuries sustained while participating in sports and, as such, is not a single career but a group of careers that is concerned with the health of the athlete. For its specific purposes, the field of sports medicine defines "athlete" as both the amateur athlete who exercises for health and recreation, and the elite athlete who is involved in sports at the college, Olympic, or professional level. People of all ages and abilities are included, including those with disabilities.

Among the professions in the field of sports medicine are the trainer, physical therapist, physiologist, biomechanical engineer, nutritionist, psychologist, and physician. In addition, the field of sports medicine also encompasses the work of those who conduct research to determine the causes of sports injuries. Discoveries made by researchers in sports medicine have spread from orthopedics to almost every branch of medicine.

Arthroscopic surgery falls into this category. It was developed by orthopedic surgeons to see and operate on skeletal joints without a large open incision. The arthroscope itself is a slender cylinder with a series of lenses that transmit the image from the joint to the eye. The lens system is surrounded by glass fibers designed to transfer light from an external source to the joint. Inserted into the joint through one small, dime- to quarter-sized incision, the arthroscope functions as the surgeon's "eyes" to allow pinpoint accuracy when operating. The surgical elements, themselves, are inserted through other small incisions nearby. In the 1970s the techniques of arthroscopy were used by only a few surgeons as an exploratory measure to determine whether or not traditional, open surgery had a good chance of succeeding. Today, arthroscopy is the most commonly performed orthopedic surgery performed in the United States, and instead of being an exploratory procedure, 80 percent of all arthroscopic surgeries are performed to repair tissue damage.

THE JOB

Sports physicians treat the injuries and illnesses of both the amateur and elite athlete. They are often referred to as *team physicians*. Depending upon the level of athlete they are treating, sports physicians are usually either practitioners in family practice as medical doctors (M.D.'s) or orthopedic surgeons. More often than not, the individual who works as the team physician for a professional sports team is too busy tending to the health needs of the team to have time for a private practice as well.

Brent Rich, M.D., head team physician for Arizona State University and team physician for the Arizona Diamondbacks, agrees that there are some varieties of sports physicians: "Sports physicians come in two major varieties: primary care providers with training in non-surgical sports medicine and orthopedic surgeons. The majority of sports physicians are in private practice. Each area has its rewards and downfalls. As a board certified family physician, I deal with about 90 percent of what goes on in the sports medicine arena."

At the scholastic level, the team physician is usually the school physician and is appointed by the school board. Athletic programs at the collegiate level are usually capable of supporting a staff of one or more physicians who cater to the needs of the athletic teams. The size of the school and athletic program also determines the number of full-time physicians; for example, a state university basketball team might have one physician, even an orthopedic surgeon, dedicated wholly to that team's needs.

Professional teams, of course, have the necessary resources to employee both a full-time physician and an orthopedic surgeon. Generally, their presence is required at all practices and games. Often, professional teams have a sports medicine department to handle the various aspects of treatment, from training to nutrition to mental health. If they don't have their own department, they take advantage of the specialists at university hospitals and private care facilities in the area.

To fully understand the nature of a particular sports injury, sports physicians study the athlete as well as the sport. The musculoskeletal system is a complex organization of muscle segments, each related to the function of others through connecting bones and articulations. Pathological states of the musculoskeletal system are reflected in deficits (weaknesses in key muscle segments) that may actually be quite distant from the site of the injury or trauma. The risk factors for any given sport can be assessed by comparing the performance demands that regularly produce characteristic injuries with the risk factors that might predispose an athlete to injury.

Strength and flexibility, for example, are requirements for nearly every sport. Stronger muscles improve an athlete's performance, and deficits in strength can leave him or her prone to injury. Rehabilitation under the supervision of a sports physician focuses on rebuilding lost muscle strength. Likewise, an athlete who lacks flexibility may subject him or herself to strains or pulls on his or her muscles. For this athlete, rehabilitation would center on warming and stretching the isolated muscles, as well as muscle groups, to reduce or alleviate such muscle strains. In both cases, it is the responsibility of the sports physician to analyze the potential for injury and work with other sports health professionals to prevent it, as well as to treat the injury after it happens. The goal of every sports physician is to keep athletes performing to the best of their ability and to rehabilitate them safely and quickly after they are injured.

To prevent injuries, as well as treat them, sports physicians administer or supervise physical examinations of the athletes under their care to determine the fitness level of each athlete prior to that athlete actively pursuing the sport. During the exams, sports physicians note any physical traits, defects, previous injuries, or weaknesses. They also check the player's maturity, coordination, stamina, balance, strength, and emotional state. The physical examination accomplishes many different goals. To begin with, it quickly establishes the athlete's state of health and allows the sports physician to determine whether that athlete is physically capable of playing his or her sport. On the basis of the physical exam, the sports physician advises the coach on the fitness level of the athlete which, of course, determines a great deal about the athlete's position on the team. Furthermore, the exam alerts the sports physician to signs of injury, both old and new. Old or existing injuries can be noted and put under observation, and weaknesses can be detected early on so that proper conditioning and training patterns can be implemented by the coach and trainers.

Depending upon the results of their physical examinations, the sports physician may advise athletes to gain or lose weight, change their eating, drinking, and sleeping habits, or alter their training programs to include more strength or cardiovascular exercises. Routine physical checkups are also a common way of evaluating an athlete's performance level throughout a season, and many sports physicians will administer several exams to gauge the effect of their advice, as well as to ensure that the athlete is making the suggested changes in habits or training.

Preventing injuries is the sports physician's first goal and conditioning is probably the best way to accomplish that goal. Sports physicians are often responsible for developing and supervising the conditioning and training programs that other sports health professionals will implement. The sports physician may work with the coaching staff and athletic trainers to help athletes develop strength, cardiovascular fitness, and flexibility, or the sports physician may advise the coaching and training staff members of the overall safety of a practice program. For example, the sports physician may evaluate the drills and practice exercises that a football coach is using on a given day to make certain that the exercises won't exacerbate old injuries or cause new ones. Sports physicians may even be involved in the selection of protective gear and equipment. The degree of their involvement, again, depends on the size of the team and the nature of the physicians' skills or expertise, as well as on the number of other people on the staff. Large, professional teams tend to have equally large staffs on which one person alone is responsible for ordering and maintaining the protective gear, for example.

Sports physicians are often in attendance at practices (or they are nearby, in case of an injury), but their presence at games is mandatory. If a player shows signs of undue fatigue, exhaustion, or injury, the sports physician needs to be there to remove the athlete from the competition. Dr. Rich says being at the games is one of the perks of his profession: "To see others accomplish what they desire gives me satisfaction. Another good part is covering sports events and feeling a part of the action on the sidelines, in the locker room, or in the heat of the battle."

After an athlete is injured, the sports physician must be capable of immediately administering first-aid or other procedures. He or she first examines the athlete to determine the gravity and extent of the injury. If the damage is extreme enough (or cannot be determined from a manual and visual exam), the sports physician may send the athlete to the hospital for X rays or other diagnostic examinations. Later, the team physician may perform surgery, or recommend that the athlete undergo treatment or surgery by a specialist. Some of the most common types of injuries are stress fractures, knee injuries, back injuries, shoulder injuries, and elbow injuries.

The sports physician oversees the athlete's recuperation and rehabilitation following an injury, including the nature and timing of physical therapy. The athlete's return to practice and competition is determined by the sports physician's analysis of the athlete's progress. Frequent physical examinations allow the physician to judge whether or not the athlete is fit enough to return to full activity. The decision to allow an athlete to compete again following an injury is a responsibility that sports physicians take seriously; whether the athlete is an amateur or an elite professional, the future health and well-being of the athlete is at stake and cannot be risked, even for an important championship game.

A developing area of the sports physician's responsibilities is the diagnosis and treatment of substance abuse problems. Unfortunately, even as research on the field of sports medicine has produced new methods and medications that mask pain and decrease inflammation—which shortens recovery time and lengthens athletic careers—some also produce unnatural performance enhancement. Most notable of these are anabolic steroids—synthetic modifications of the male hormone, testosterone—which have become widely abused by athletes who use them to better their performances. When taken while on a high protein diet and an intensive exercise regimen, these drugs can increase muscle bulk, which in turn can produce increased strength, speed, and stamina. The side effects of these drugs, however, include aggression, sterility, liver problems, premature closure of the growth plates of the long bones, and in women, male pattern baldness and facial hair.

These side effects are usually irreversible and, as such, pose a significant health risk for young athletes.

Another method also banned from use in competition-level athletics is the withdrawal of an athlete's blood several weeks prior to competition. The blood is stored and then, just before the athlete competes, the blood is transfused back into his or her bloodstream. This process, blood doping, also has serious, even fatal, side effects, including heart failure and death.

Finally, professional athletes sometimes develop substance abuse problems, such as alcohol or drug use. Sports physicians are responsible for detecting all of these problems and helping the athlete return to a healthy lifestyle, which may include competition.

In addition to the responsibilities and duties outlined above, many sports physicians also perform clinical studies and work with researchers to determine ways of improving sports medicine practices. Often, the results of such studies and research are published in medical journals and even popular magazines.

REQUIREMENTS

High School

During high school, take as many health and sports-related classes as possible. Biology, chemistry, health, computers, and English are important core courses. High grades in high school are important for anyone aspiring to join the medical profession, because competition for acceptance into medical programs at colleges and universities is always tough.

Postsecondary Training

Sports physicians have either an M.D. (medical doctor degree) or a D.O. (doctor of osteopathy degree). Each involves completing four years of college, followed by four years of medical school, study and internship at an accredited medical school, and up to six years of residency training in a medical specialty, such as surgery. Many physicians also complete a fellowship in sports medicine either during or after their residency.

During the first two years of medical school, students usually spend most of their time in classrooms learning anatomy, physiology, biology, and chemistry, among other subjects. In their last two years, they begin seeing patients in a clinic, observing and working with doctors to treat patients and develop their diagnostic skills. Some medical schools are beginning to alter this time-honored tradition by having medical students begin to work with patients much sooner than two years into their schooling, but this method of combining classroom and clinical experiences is not yet fully accepted or integrated into the curriculum.

After medical school, the new doctors spend a year in an internship program, followed by several years in a residency training program in their area of specialty. Most sports physicians complete this stage of their training by working in orthopedics or general practice.

The fellowship portion of a doctor's training is essential if he or she has chosen to specialize. For example, the doctor specializing in general surgery and interested in sports medicine would probably seek an orthopedics fellowship providing further training in orthopedic surgery techniques.

Certification or Licensing

To become licensed, doctors must have completed the above training in accordance with the guidelines and rules of their chosen area or specialty. Beyond the formal requirements, this usually involves a qualifying written exam, followed by in-depth oral examinations designed to test the candidate's knowledge and expertise.

Other Requirements

To be a successful sports physician, you must be able to learn and remember all the many parts and variations about the human body and how it functions. Knowledge of different sports and their demands on an athlete's body is also important. Like all medical doctors, you need to be able to communicate clearly to your patients with compassion and understanding.

EXPLORING

High school students interested in becoming sports physicians should look into the possibility of working with the physician, coach, or athletic trainer for one of their school's teams. Firsthand experience is the best way to gain fresh perspective into the role of the team physician. Later on, when applying for other paid or volunteer positions, it will help to have already had sports-related experience. Dr. Rich agrees, "Try to get experience with a physician who does what you think you want to do. Spending time in their offices, in surgery, or on the sidelines at high school games will give you exposure. As you learn more, you can do more."

EMPLOYERS

Most sports physicians are in private practice, so they work for themselves or with other medical doctors. Some sports physicians, however, may work for sports clinics, rehabilitation centers, hospitals, and college/university teaching hospitals. Still other sports physicians travel with professional baseball, basketball, football, hockey, and soccer teams to attend to those specific athletes. Sports physicians are employed all over the country.

STARTING OUT

You won't become the team physician for a National Basketball Association team fresh out of medical school. Many sports physicians begin by joining an existing practice and volunteering with a local sports organization. After several years they may apply to the school board for consideration as a team physician for their local school district. Later, they may apply for a position with a college team until they ultimately seek a position with a national or international professional athletics team or organization. This gradual climb occurs while the individual also pursues a successful private practice and builds a strong, solid reputation. Often, the sports physician's established reputation in an area of specialty draws the attention of coaches and management looking to hire a physician for their team. Others take a more aggressive and ambitious route and immediately begin applying for positions with various professional sports teams as an assistant team physician. As in any other field, contacts can prove to be extremely useful, as are previous experiences in the field. For example, a summer volunteership or internship during high school or college with a professional hockey team might lead to a job possibility with that hockey team years later. Employment opportunities depend on the skill and ambitions of each job candidate.

ADVANCEMENT

Depending on the nature of an aspiring sports physician's affiliation with athletic organizations (part time or full time), advancement paths will vary. For most sports physicians, advancement will accompany the successful development of their private practices. For those few sports physicians who are employed full time by professional athletic organizations, advancement from assistant to team physician is usually accompanied by increased responsibilities and a corresponding increase in salary.

EARNINGS

The earnings of a sports physician vary depending upon his or her responsibilities and the size and nature of the team. The private sports physician of a professional individual athlete, such as a figure skater or long distance runner, will most likely earn far less than the team physician for a professional football or basketball team, primarily because the earnings of the team are so much greater so the organization can afford to pay more for the physician's services. On the other hand, the team physician for the professional basketball team probably wouldn't have time for a private practice, although the sports physician for the figure skater or runner would, in all likelihood, also have a private practice or work for a sports health facility.

According to the U.S. Department of Labor, general practitioners and family practice physicians earn an annual net income of approximately $118,400 in 2001. Ten percent of these physicians earned less than $46,700 annually in that same year. This general figure does not include the fees and other income sports physicians receive from the various athletic organizations for whom they work. Again, these fees will vary according to the size of the team, the location, and the level of the athletic organization (high school, college, or professional, being the most common). The income generated from these fees is far less than what they earn in their private practices. On the other hand, those team physicians who are employed full time by a professional organization will likely make more than their nonprofessional sports counterparts, even as much as $1 million or more.

WORK ENVIRONMENT

Sports physicians must be ready for a variety of work conditions, from the sterile, well-lighted hospital operating room to the concrete bleachers at an outdoor municipal swimming pool. The work environment is as diverse as the sports in which athletes are involved. Although most of their day-to-day responsibilities will be carried out in clean, comfortable surroundings, on game day sports physicians are expected to be where the athletes are, and that might be a muddy field (football and soccer), a snow-covered forest (cross-country skiing), a hot, dusty track (track and field), or a steamy ring (boxing). Picture the playing field of any given sport and that is where you will find sports physicians. They are also expected to travel with the athletes whenever they go out of town. This means being away from their home and family, often for several days, depending on the nature, level, and location of the competition.

OUTLOOK

After years of watching athletes close down the bars after a game, coaches and management now realize the benefits of good health and nutrition. Within the world of professional sports, the word is out: proper nutrition, conditioning, and training prevent injuries to athletes, and preventing injuries is the key when those athletes are making their owners revenues in the billions of dollars. A top sports physician, then, is a worthwhile investment for any professional team. Thus, the outlook for sports physicians remains strong.

Even outside the realm of professional sports, amateur athletes require the skills and expertise of talented sports physicians to handle the aches and pains that come from pulling muscles and overtaxing aging knees. Athletes of all ages and abilities take their competitions seriously, and are as prone to injury as any pro athlete, if not more, because amateur athletes in general spend less time conditioning their bodies.

FOR MORE INFORMATION

To obtain publications about sports medicine, contact
American College of Sports Medicine
PO Box 1440
401 West Michigan Street
Indianapolis, IN 46206-1440
Tel: 317-637-9200
http://www.acsm.org

To join a forum on various medical issues, visit the AMA's website
American Medical Association (AMA)
515 North State Street
Chicago, IL 60610
Tel: 312-464-5000
http://www.ama-assn.org

For general information on sports medicine, contact
American Orthopaedic Society for Sports Medicine
6300 North River Road, Suite 500
Rosemont, IL 60018

Tel: 847-292-4900
Email: aossm@aossm.org
http://www.sportsmed.org

For a list of accredited athletic training programs, job listings, and information on certification for athletic trainers, contact
National Athletic Trainers' Association
2952 Stemmons Freeway
Dallas, TX 75247-6916
Tel: 214-637-6282
Email: membership@nata.org
http://www.nata.org

Sports Psychologists

OVERVIEW

In general, *sports psychologists* work with amateur and professional athletes to improve their mental and physical health and athletic performances by using goal setting, imagery, attentional focus strategies, and relaxation techniques, among others. Sports psychologists also strive to help athletes to mentally prepare for competition. There are approximately 182,000 psychologists employed in the United States, but sports psychologists comprise only a small segment of this number.

HISTORY

In the 17th century, René Descartes described his belief that human behaviors could be classified in two ways—voluntary and involuntary. Those behaviors that were completely mechanical, instinctual, and similar to those of animals, he characterized as involuntary; those behaviors that required or submitted to reason were characterized as voluntary. Based on this early model, and the subsequent work of others, including John Locke, James Mill, and John Stuart Mill, later philosophers and scientists experimented with sensation and perception, culminating with an introspective analysis of the many elements of an individual's experience.

William James advanced modern psychology by asserting the theory of a stream of thought and G. Stanley Hall, a contemporary of James, established the first true laboratory of psychology at Clark University in 1883. Sigmund Freud introduced the medical tradition to clinical psychology. A physician and neurologist, Freud's methods of psychoanalysis included word association techniques and, later, inkblot techniques as developed by Hermann Rorschach.

After World War II, psychology was recognized as a formal profession, the American Psychological Association (APA) developed standards of training, and certification and licensing laws were passed to regulate the practice of professional psychology.

Since psychology deals with human behavior, psychologists apply their knowledge and techniques to a wide range of endeavors including human services, management, law, and sports.

THE JOB

Sport and exercise psychology is the scientific study of the psychological factors that are associated with participation and performance in sport, exercise, and other types of physical activity. Sports psychologists are divided into three categories: clinical, educational, and research. *Clinical sports psychologists* work mainly with individuals who are experiencing emotional problems that are usually, but not always, somehow connected to their sport. *Educational sports psychologists* have two roles, one as a classroom instructor and the other as a consultant. In the classroom, they teach students methods and techniques related to sports psychology. On the field, they usually function as members of the coaching staff. Just as the coach teaches physical skills, the sports psychologist teaches mental skills. *Research sports psychologists* conduct studies that provide the clinical and educational sports psychologists with scientific facts and statistics.

All sport psychology professionals are interested in two main objectives: helping athletes use psychological principles to improve performance (performance enhancement) and understanding how participation in sport, exercise, and physical activity affects an individual's psychological development, health, and well-being throughout the life span.

Sports psychologists work with individual athletes and entire teams. They may concentrate on the problems the athlete is having with the sport, from a bad slump to the feelings of low self-esteem that come when the crowd jeers the athlete's performance. They also work to help the individual athlete to overcome feelings of depression, drug or substance abuse, and violence.

Sports psychologists also work with teams in many ways, the most notable of which is creating a feeling of cohesion among the many different personalities that constitute a team. Team members are also counseled when they are traded to another team or released. Sports psychologists also work with individual athletes and team members on improving their level of performance, concentration, and mental attitude. The phrase "a winning attitude" derives its power from the fact that sports psychologists can help the athletes with whom they work to actually visualize a winning shot or a perfect golf swing and then execute that vision.

Sports psychologists don't work with only exceptional, elite athletes or teams; in fact, most sports psychologists work with college athletes or amateur athletes, and many teach in academic settings or offer their own, motivational lecture series. Some sports psychologists have their own columns in specialized sports magazines and others work in athletic training facilities, hired full time by the owners to work with the athletes who come to train there.

REQUIREMENTS

The requirements for entering the field of sports medicine as a sports psychologist are somewhat tricky to understand, so it helps to understand the various paths available in psychology in general, as determined by the APA. Students should expect to spend five to seven years in graduate work if they are interested in pursuing doctoral degrees.

High School

High school students should take a college preparatory curriculum that concentrates on English, mathematics, and sciences. You should also take a foreign language, especially French and German, because reading comprehension of these languages is one of the usual requirements for obtaining a doctoral degree. Participation in sports will give you the background necessary to effectively understand the athletes you work with in your practice.

Postsecondary Training

A doctoral degree is generally required for employment as a psychologist, but there are two different degrees that psychologists can seek at the doctorate level. The first degree is called the Ph.D., and psychologists with this degree qualify for a wide range of teaching, research, clinical, and counseling positions in universities, elementary and secondary schools, and private industry. The second degree is called a Psy.D. (Doctor of Psychology), and psychologists with this degree qualify mainly for clinical positions. The Ph.D. degree culminates in a dissertation based on original research, while the Psy.D. degree is usually based on practical work and examinations rather than a dissertation. In clinical or counseling psychology, the requirements for a doctoral degree usually include a year or more of internship or supervised experience.

Individuals who have only a master's degree in psychology are allowed to administer tests as psychological assistants and, if they are under the supervision of doctoral-level psychologists they can conduct research in laboratories, conduct psychological evaluations, counsel patients, and perform administrative duties. They are also allowed to teach in high schools and two-year colleges and work as school psychologists or counselors.

Those individuals with only a bachelor's degree in psychology can assist psychologists and other professionals and work as research or administrative assistants, but without further academic training, they cannot advance further in psychology.

Having said all of this, it will perhaps come as a shock that there no sports psychology doctoral programs accredited by the APA. One of the controversies behind this is whether professionals working with athletes in applied areas of sports psychology should be required to have doctoral training in clinical or counseling psychology—training that would qualify them to provide psychological treatment to athletes as well. The solution reached by the APA, along with the Association for the Advancement of Applied Sports Psychology (AAASP) and North American Society for the Psychology of Sport and Physical Activity, is that any practitioners of sports psychology who do not also have doctoral-level clinical or counseling training should refer athletes who need treatment to licensed professionals. Sports psychologists who work with Olympic athletes are required to have doctoral-level degrees.

Those students who are interested in academic teaching and research in sports psychology can earn doctoral degrees in sport sciences and take additional courses in psychology or counseling. Over 50 schools in the United States offer this type of program, including the University of North Carolina-Greensboro (http://www.uncg.edu) and the University of Florida (http://www.ufl.edu). Typical subjects covered include sports psychology, performance enhancement, concentration skills, stress and attention management, and motivation.

Those students who want more emphasis on psychology in their training can pursue a psychology doctorate in areas such as group procedures, psychotherapy, learning, education, and human development or motivation, with a subspecialty in sports psychology. At most universities, students take courses like these in the sport sciences department, while at a few schools, such as the University of Washington (http://www.washington.edu) and the University of

California-Los Angeles (http://www.ucla.edu), it is possible to take similar courses through the psychology department.

Students who wish to provide clinical services to athletes can pursue a doctoral degree in APA-accredited clinical or counseling psychology programs, with a concentration in sports psychology. This track offers students the widest range of job opportunities, from teaching and research in sports and psychology to counseling athletes as well as the general population. Institutions where this mode of study is typical include the University of Wisconsin-Madison (http://www.wisc.edu) and the University of North Texas (http://www.unt.edu).

For those students who are interested primarily in educating people about the health benefits of exercise or in helping student athletes, a master's degree is an option. More than 100 sport sciences departments offer a master's degree in areas related to sports psychology.

For more detailed information on graduate programs in psychology and sports psychology, look for *The Directory of Graduate Programs in Applied Sport Psychology*, available from the APA.

Certification or Licensing

In addition to educational requirements, most states require that all practitioners of psychology meet certification or licensing requirements if they are in independent practice or involved in offering patient care of any kind (including clinical and counseling). Once the educational requirements are fulfilled, a sports psychologist should contact the AAASP for details about certification and licensing requirements, as they usually vary from state to state.

Other Requirements

Because sports psychology is such a broad field, various personal attributes apply to different psychology positions. Clinical sports psychologists should be able to relate to others and have excellent listening skills. Educational sports psychologists should have strong communication skills in order to convey ideas and concepts to students and clients. Research sports psychologists should be analytical, detail oriented, and have strong writing and mathematics skills.

EXPLORING

You can gain experience in this field by volunteering to work for research programs at area universities or by working in the office of a psychologist. Another option is to learn more about sports by

Visualization Works

Sports psychologists have long instructed their athletic clients to use positive imagery, or visualization, when training to improve performance. But how does it work?

Our brains not only store information on how to breathe, walk, eat, and talk, but they also store information on running fast, jumping high, or whatever athletic task is at hand. But to be able to retrieve this information, athletes need to practice using it.

For example, a runner may use imagery by visualizing the act of passing a competitor, feeling strong, and maintaining a quick pace. The runner should practice this method while training, visualizing the passing of the next tree, for example. Then, when used in a race, visualization can be used to build confidence and encourage maximum effort.

When used most simply, visualization can be used as a substitute for training, such as when an athlete is injured or otherwise unable to physically exercise. However, when imagery is combined with training, the results are much more effective.

Source: Mind Tools (http://www.mindtools.org)

working as a gofer or intern with the sports medicine departments of college, university, or professional athletic teams. Even by participating in a sport in high school or college, you can gain valuable insight into the mental and emotional stresses and demands placed upon athletes.

In addition, students should begin their understanding of psychology by taking as many courses in the field as possible.

EMPLOYERS

Sports psychologists are employed by athletes at the amateur, college, and professional levels, and by owners of professional, college, and private organizations. They may also be employed at colleges and universities as teachers and researchers.

STARTING OUT

Along the road toward a Ph.D. or Psy.D., students of all levels can get involved in the research or educational aspects of psychology, either as a volunteer subject or a paid helper. These positions will gradually increase in responsibility and scope as the student progresses in his or her studies. Eventually, the student will be eligible for internships that will, in turn, provide him or her with valuable contacts in the field.

Graduates can explore job opportunities with a wide variety of employers, from the university research branch of psychology or sport sciences to the world of elite athletes. Finding work with the latter, however, can prove extremely difficult.

ADVANCEMENT

Sports psychologists advance in several ways, but they do so primarily by increasing the scope and caliber of their reputations in the field. This is accomplished, of course, by consistently helping athletes to improve their athletic performance and to reduce the emotional and/or mental strain placed upon them. Advancement might come in the form of a new position (working for a professional team) or it might come in the form of a solid, private practice.

Sports psychologists who make their living largely in the academic world do so by successfully publishing the results of studies, research, or theories in specialized medical journals.

EARNINGS

Specific salary figures for sports psychologists are not readily available, but psychologists in general can earn any where from $22,000 to $200,000, depending the area of their expertise, the location of their practice, and whether or not they practice alone or in a partnership. Be forewarned, however, that with the higher salary comes long years of study in order to attain the educational background necessary to practice. In fact, in order to stay current with topics ranging from treatment to medication, psychologists must continue to learn and study their field for as long as they intend to practice.

WORK ENVIRONMENT

Sports psychologists spend most of their time working in office and hospital environments, but some of their time is spent in the same environments as the athletes they counsel. This may mean spending several hours on a golf course, on a ski slope, or in the gymnasium. Much depends on the type of psychologist. For example, the clinical psychologist would probably spend most of his or her time with athletes in the relative comfort of an office setting and the psychologist would meet with athletes during a regular, nine-to-five day. Educational sports psychologists would be more likely to be in the gym or on the golf course, working side-by-side with the rest of the coaching staff. Finally, depending on the nature of the study, a research sports psychologist might spend some time with the athletes while they were practicing, but in general, the research psychologist would spend most of his or her time in an office or laboratory setting, reviewing or studying the data from his or her studies.

Sports psychologists need to stay up-to-date with developing theories and research and to accomplish this, they may have to spend additional time reading journals, books, and papers; conducting research in the library; or attending conferences on relevant issues. They may need to take additional course work to stay abreast of new theories and techniques, as well as to maintain current certification or licensing. Although sports psychologists spend a lot of time with the athletes they're helping, they also spend large amounts of time working alone.

OUTLOOK

While employment in the field of psychology in general is likely to grow about as fast as the average for all occupations over the next several years, it is hard to say how this prognosis affects sports psychology. Very few people leave the field entirely, which is largely due to the fact that so much time goes into training. Many stay in the general field of psychology and merely move around, switching specialties, but even this is rare.

While competition is incredibly tough for positions with elite athletes, most experts believe that other areas of sports psychology will continue to offer a substantial number of jobs to new graduates, especially in academe.

Sports psychology may, at first, seem lucrative, but it can lack the steady income of a private practice or academic teaching post because practitioners are frequently only on call, not steadily billing for their time. It can also be difficult to get work because while they might have a famous athlete for a client, the chances are pretty good that the athlete doesn't want it known that he or she is getting counseling for a bad marriage, a slump, or a drug problem. This forces the sports psychologist to rely on referrals that, again, might not happen all that often when athletes and their agents are trying to keep the athlete's therapy a secret.

FOR MORE INFORMATION

For information on career options in psychology, contact
American Psychological Association
750 First Street, NE
Washington, DC 20002-4242
Tel: 800-374-2721
http://www.apa.org

For certification info and an overview of the field, visit the What is
Sport Psychology? *section of the AAASP website.*
**Association for the Advancement of Applied Sports Psychology
(AAASP)**
801 Main Street, Suite 010
Louisville, CO 80027
Tel: 303-494-5931
http://www.aaasponline.org

Sports Trainers

OVERVIEW

Sports trainers, also referred to as *athletic trainers, certified sports medicine trainers,* and *certified sports medicine therapists,* help amateur and professional athletes prevent injuries, give first aid when an injury occurs during a practice or event, and manage the rehabilitation programs and routines of injured athletes.

Athletic trainers often consult with physicians during all stages of athletic training to ensure that athletes under their care are physically capable of participating in competition. In addition, they specialize in health care administration, education, and counseling. There are approximately 12,580 athletic trainers employed in the United States.

HISTORY

Aristotle, Leonardo da Vinci, and Etienne Jules Marey all conducted experiments and studies involving motion and the human body, but it was the French physiologist Marey whose devices to study human motion really advanced the field of biomechanics and sports medicine. In fact, both modern cinematography and sports medicine claim him as the father of their respective fields. Marey's first contribution was the first force platform, a device which was able to visualize the forces between the foot and the floor. Later, his nonphotographic studies of the gait of a horse inspired Eadward Muybridge's serial photographs of a horse in motion in 1877, which, in turn, inspired Marey's invention of the chronophotograph. In contrast to Muybridge's consecutive frames, taken by several cameras, Marey's pictures with the chronophotograph superimposed the stages of action onto a single photograph, giving form to motion and allowing scientists to study it frame by frame, motion by motion. By 1892, Marey had even made primitive motion pictures, but his efforts were quickly eclipsed by those of Louis and Auguste Lumiere.

Following both World Wars I and II, Marey's and other scientists' experiments with motion would combine with medicine's need to heal and/or completely replace the limbs of war veterans. In order to provide an amputee with a prosthetic device that would come as close as possible to replicating the movement and functional value of a real limb, scientists and doctors began to work together to understand the range of motion peculiar to the human body.

Mechanically, sports can be categorized according to the kinds of movements used. Each individual sport utilizes a unique combination of basic motions, including walking, running, jumping, kicking, and throwing. These basic motions have all been rigidly defined for scientific study so that injuries related to these motions can be better understood and treated. For example, sports that place heavy demands on one part of an athlete's body may overload that part and produce an injury, such as "tennis elbow" and "swimmer's shoulder." Baseball, on the other hand, is a throwing sport and certain injuries from overuse of the shoulder and elbow are expected. Athletes who play volleyball or golf also use some variation of the throwing motion and therefore, also sustain injuries to their shoulders and elbows.

Today, sports trainers are part of the team of sports medicine professionals that treat the injuries of both the amateur and elite athlete. Like sports physicians, certified sports medicine therapists are responsible for preventing injuries as well as treating them, and they use their knowledge of the human body and its wide range of motions to discover new ways of reducing stress and damage from athletic activities. They work in high schools, secondary schools, colleges and universities, and a smaller number work for professional teams. Many work in health clubs, sports medicine clinics, and other athletic health care settings. In 1990, the American Medical Association (AMA) recognized athletic training as an allied health profession.

THE JOB

Sports trainers help amateur and professional athletes prevent injuries through proper exercises and conditioning, provide immediate first-aid attention to injuries as they occur during a practice or event, and lead injured athletes safely through rehabilitation programs and routines. For the most part, sports trainers are not medical doctors, and they are not allowed to conduct certain procedures or provide advanced types of medical care, such as prescribing or administering drugs. Some trainers, however, are trained physicians. If an individual is also trained as an *osteopathic physician,* for example, he or she is licensed as a medical doctor and can conduct more advanced procedures and techniques, including diagnosis, surgery, and the prescription of drugs.

In order to prevent injuries, sports trainers organize team physicals, making certain that each player is examined and evaluated by a physician prior to that athlete's participation in the sport. Along with the team physician, they help to analyze each athlete's overall readiness to play, fitness level, and known or existing weaknesses or injuries. When necessary, they recommend stretching, conditioning, and strengthening exercises to aid the athlete in preventing or exacerbating an injury. This may involve developing specific routines for individual athletes. Finally, athletic trainers work with coaches, and sometimes team physicians, to choose protective athletic equipment. Before games and practice, they often inspect the playing field, surface, or area for any flagrant or subtle risks of injury to the athlete.

Prior to a practice or competition, the athletic trainer may help an athlete conduct special stretching exercises or, as a preventive measure, he or she might tape, wrap, bandage, or brace knees, ankles, or other joints, and areas of the athlete's body that might be at risk for injury. The trainer routinely treats cuts, scratches, and abrasions, among other minor injuries. He or she may tape, pad, or wrap injuries, and install face guards. When serious injuries do occur, whether in practice or during a competition, the athletic trainer's role is to provide prompt and accurate first-aid treatment to the athlete to ensure that athlete's full recovery. He or she is trained in emergency procedures and is prepared to provide emergency treatment for conditions such as shock, concussion, or bone fracture, stabilizing the athlete until they reach a hospital or trauma center. Often, the trainer will accompany the injured athlete to the hospital, making certain the team physician is still on hand to address the health concerns and needs of those athletes who are still competing.

Working in concert with the team physician and several other health professionals, athletic trainers often supervise the therapeutic rehabilitation of athletes under their care. They analyze the athlete's injury and create individualized therapy routines. Sometimes, the trainer may advise the athlete to wear a protective brace or guard to minimize damage while the athlete is recuperating from an injury. Athletic trainers in charge of every level of athlete should be licensed to perform specific medical functions and operate certain devices and equipment.

REQUIREMENTS

High School

If you have an interest in becoming a sports trainer, you've probably already become involved in the field during high school. Maybe you're not an athlete but you work as a trainer or manager for one of your school teams. These are excellent ways to develop your interest in sports, learn about the skills that trainers must have, and develop the leadership abilities necessary for the job.

If you're interested in this field, you should pay special attention to physical education classes and to high school subjects such as health and anatomy and physiology. Students with an interest in becoming athletic trainers will want to become certified in CPR and first aid.

Postsecondary Training

Sports trainers usually earn a bachelor's degree from a college or university that offers a program in athletic training which is accredited by the Joint Review Committee on Educational Programs in Athletic Training. Later, you will intern with a certified athletic trainer. Another option is to earn a bachelor's degree or even a master's degree in a related health field, such as osteopathy, and then intern with a certified athletic trainer. The number of hours you need to spend in both clinical study and in the internship phase will vary, depending on the program you select and the professional organization that you decide to join.

Most accredited programs in athletic training include course work in the prevention and evaluation of athletic injuries and illnesses, first aid and emergency care, therapeutic exercises, therapeutic modalities, administration of athletic training programs, human anatomy, human physiology, exercise physiology, kinesiology, nutrition, psychology, and personal and community health.

Certification or Licensing

As mentioned earlier, athletic trainers in charge of every level of athlete should be licensed to perform specific medical functions and operate certain devices and equipment. Different membership organizations and their respective certifying bodies have different eligibility requirements; it is up to you to decide which organization best characterizes your ultimate goal.

For example, the National Athletic Trainers' Association (NATA) requires that each member have a bachelor's degree (in any field), be either a graduate of an accredited program in athletic training (with

800 clinical hours) or complete an internship (with 1,500 clinical hours), and pass a certification exam consisting of three sections—written, simulation, and oral practical.

Approximately 41 states require some form of certification, licensure, or registration for athletic trainers. For more information, check with your state's regulatory agency in the state in which you would like to practice for more information.

Other Requirements

Workers in this field need an understanding of human anatomy and physiology, both in terms of physical capabilities and injury treatment and prevention. You should not be squeamish when it comes to blood, broken bones, or other wounds. Athletes do get hurt, and a trainer who is unable to cope well with this aspect of sports may have a difficult time succeeding in the career. The ability and knowledge to handle medical emergencies is especially important for certified athletic trainers, whose work focuses on injury prevention and treatment.

EXPLORING

Most trainers, like other professionals who work with athletes, were first drawn to sports as participants. High school and college students can gain valuable experience by actively participating in a sport. Such experience lends a prospective trainer added insight into the injuries typical of a given sport, as well as the compassion and empathy necessary to comfort an injured athlete who is forced to sit out a game. Most teams need help with everything from equipment to statistics, so plenty of opportunities exist to explore a variety of sports-related positions. If you are certain about becoming an athletic trainer, you can often work with a trainer or team physician, learning beside a professional. This type of experience will come in handy, later, when you are looking for an internship or a job; successful candidates are usually those with the most experience and on-the-job training.

EMPLOYERS

Sports trainers are employed by professional and amateur sports teams, private sports organizations, sports facilities, educational institutions, and by individual athletes. Other possible athletic training employment opportunities include corporate health programs, health clubs, clinical and industrial health care programs, and athletic training curriculum programs.

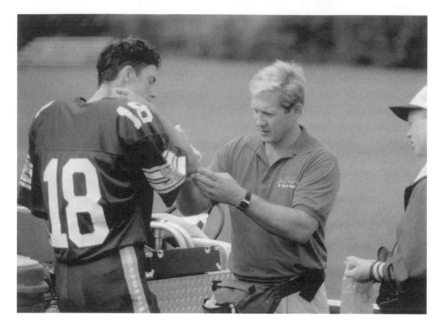

A sports trainer tends to a player's injury. (*Jim Whitmer Photography*)

STARTING OUT

Athletic trainers, regardless of the professional organization they join, are usually required to complete a period of training with a certified athletic trainer or sports medicine therapist. These internships provide students with the foundation for future networking possibilities. Many students find full-time jobs with the teams, organizations, or school districts with which they interned. At the very least, these internships offer students the chance to make valuable contacts and gain valuable on-the-job experience.

Most accredited programs in athletic training also have job placement departments that host recruitment seminars with major organizations, provide career counseling services, and put students in contact with prospective employers.

Finally, one of the benefits to belonging to a professional organization is that these associations publish newsletters and maintain websites, both of which feature job openings. Some organizations even offer job hotlines to their members. Through these media, as well as through meetings, seminars, and continuing education, students and trainers can make new contacts that will help them locate work and add to their base of knowledge. NATA, for example, boasts the most comprehensive job referral service in the United States for athletic trainers, listing job openings in all athletic training settings and locations.

ADVANCEMENT

Acquiring additional training and education is the most common way of advancing in the field of sports training. Those trainers who have spent years working in the field and who update their skills each year by taking continuing education courses, sometimes even returning to school for an advanced degree, will be among the first to receive promotions.

Management responsibilities are the other way in which athletic trainers can advance in their field. Large universities often employ several trainers to serve the many different teams, with one trainer acting as the head trainer, sometimes also called the *director of sports medicine*. This individual coordinates the daily activities and responsibilities of the other trainers and works closely with the coaches of the school's various teams to ensure that all the demands are being met. Most often, trainers advance by working for several years at one school, and then move on to another school when an opening is announced that will mean greater responsibilities and benefits.

EARNINGS

Earnings vary depending on the level of athletics in which the trainer is involved, the trainer's education and credentials, and the number and type of his or her responsibilities. Those considering a career as an athletic trainer should keep all aspects of the job and salary in perspective; the slight increase in salary of a trainer working for a college team might be offset by the higher stress levels and longer hours away from home. Trainers who work with professional athletes are away from home a great deal, including evenings, weekends, and holidays.

According to the National Association for Sport and Physical Education, salaries for athletic trainers in schools range from $25,000 to $35,000. With experience and a master's degree, college trainers can earn up to $45,000 to $60,000 per year. Athletic trainers who work for professional sports teams earn salaries ranging from $60,000 to $125,000.

The U.S. Department of Labor reports that athletic trainers earned median salaries of $33,450 in 2001. The highest 10 percent earned more than $54,440, while the lowest 10 percent earned less than $19,330.

WORK ENVIRONMENT

Athletes train year round and so do the sports trainers who supervise their conditioning and rehabilitation programs. Depending upon the level and size of an athletic program, trainers may work with athletes in one or more sports. Sports trainers who work in high schools often act as the trainer for several, or all, of the athletic teams. A lot also depends on the school's budgetary restrictions. Generally speaking, though, most schools have a separate trainer for men's and women's sports. Trainers in professional sports work only in one sport and for one team.

Most of the trainer's time is spent in the school's athletic facility, either in preparation for work or in conditioning or rehab sessions. Athletic trainers are on a schedule similar to that of their athletes; they go to practices, schedule weight and rehab sessions, and attend games. They are expected to travel when and where the team travels.

OUTLOOK

Depending on the level of athletics in which the trainer is involved, the outlook for this career varies. Like most careers, competition for more glamorous jobs is tough; positions with professional athletes and teams are extremely difficult to find and those working in them usually have years and years of experience. More opportunities exist for certified athletic trainers who work with high school athletes, especially if trainers have other skills that make them more employable. For example, the athletic trainer wishing to work with high school athletes who also can teach biology, math, physical education, or other school subjects most likely will find a position sooner than the candidate with only a background in athletic training. The reasoning is simple: with school budgets being cut back, those individuals who perform double-duty will be more attractive to school boards looking to cut costs.

Positions at the college and university level offer the athletic trainer greater stability, with little turnover. Competition for these spots is also tough, however, and many schools are now requiring candidates to have a master's degree.

FOR MORE INFORMATION

To obtain publications about sports medicine, contact
American College of Sports Medicine
PO Box 1440
Indianapolis, IN 46206-1440
http://www.acsm.org

For a list of accredited athletic training programs, job listings, and information on certification, contact

National Athletic Trainers' Association
2952 Stemmons Freeway
Dallas, TX 75247-6916
Tel: 214-637-6282
http://www.nata.org

For information on certification, contact

National Athletic Trainers' Association Board of Certification
4223 South 143rd Circle
Omaha, NE 68137-4505
Tel: 877-262-3926
Email: staff@nataboc.org
http://www.nataboc.org

Yoga and Pilates Instructors

QUICK FACTS

School Subjects
Health
Physical education

Personal Skills
Helping/teaching
Leadership/management

Work Environment
Primarily indoors
Primarily one location

Minimum Education Level
High school diploma

Salary Range
$10/hour to $30/hour to
$250/hour

Certification or Licensing
Required for certain
positions

Outlook
Faster than the average

DOT
153

GOE
10.02.02

NOC
5254

O*NET-SOC
39-9031.00

OVERVIEW

Yoga and Pilates instructors lead specialized exercise, stretching, and meditation classes for people of all ages. They demonstrate techniques in front of the class and then watch members perform the movements, making suggestions and form adjustments as needed. Classes range from introductory to intermediate to advanced, and they may be aimed at specific groups, such as children or the elderly. Yoga instructors lead their class through a series of *asanas,* or poses, aimed at building strength, flexibility, and balance. Pilates instructors teach a more fluid series of movements than the poses used in yoga. Pilates also builds strength and flexibility but focuses on training the individual's "core," or center.

HISTORY

Yoga and Pilates have been around in other cultures for some time, but they have become more popular in the United States only in the last few decades.

Yoga, which literally means "to yoke together," is an ancient practice. According to the American Yoga Association, early stone carvings and illustrations dating back 5,000 years reveal depictions of people in yoga positions. Contrary to popular belief, yoga is not rooted in Hinduism. In fact, Hinduism was established much later, and early Hindu leaders adopted and promoted certain yoga beliefs and practices for their followers.

One of the earliest known yoga teachers and promoters was a man named Patanjali, who wrote about his yoga practice in a work called

Yoga Sutras. His writings covered the basic philosophy and techniques that later became Hatha Yoga. Within Hatha are many styles, such as Iyengar, Ashtanga, Integral, Kripalu, and Jiva Mukti. Ashtanga Yoga, one of the most popular branches, incorporates eight elements: restraint, observance, breathing exercises, physical exercises, preparation for meditation, concentration, meditation, and self-realization. Most modern yoga instructors focus on just a few of these elements, leading classes through physical poses, breathing techniques, and preparation for meditation.

Pilates, pronounced "puh-lot-eez," was developed by Joseph Pilates in the early 1900s. Since he was a German living in England during the start of World War I, Pilates was forced into a camp with other foreign nationals. During this time, Pilates encouraged his fellow cellmates to keep moving, even those who were bedridden. According to Katherine Robertson, author of *Pilates . . . the Intelligent, Elegant, Workout,* Joseph Pilates developed exercise equipment specifically for the injured, converting hospital beds to "bednasiums," which encouraged health and healing through resistance exercise.

This early rehabilitation work led to the machinery behind Pilates exercise. In addition to floor work, Joseph Pilates also incorporated complex equipment consisting of belts, loops, chains, and springs designed to strengthen and lengthen the core muscles of the body.

Today, Pilates is still practiced in its original form, with both mat work and equipment, though many instructors, because of the cost of equipment, offer classes consisting of just floor exercises.

THE JOB

Yoga and Pilates instructors teach alternative exercise methods to the more traditional aerobics, weight training, or interval training classes. With yoga, the instructors' methods vary greatly based on the type of yoga they teach. Some instructors begin class seated or even lying down, encouraging class members to relax their muscles and focus on their breathing. After a few minutes of breathing exercises, the instructor then leads the class into the various asanas, or yoga poses. These poses have Sanskrit names, though the instructor may use the English terminology for the benefit of the class, instructing students to get into the "downward dog" or "child's" pose. Again, depending on the yoga method, poses may be fluid, with quicker movement from position to position, or instructors may tell class members to hold poses for as long as three or four minutes, encouraging strength and control.

A Pilates instructor adjusts a class member's form while he uses specialized equipment. *(Corbis)*

Most yoga classes are done barefoot on the floor, using a thin, rubber mat to keep class members from slipping while in poses. Other equipment, such as foam blocks, ropes, or cloth straps, may also be used in the poses, usually to help with form or assist in the tougher positions.

During the class, yoga instructors verbally describe and demonstrate moves in front of the class. They also walk around and survey the movements of class members, making slight adjustments to members' form to prevent injury, encourage good practice, and improve their skills.

Pilates is similar to yoga in that class participants are led through different motions. However, unlike yoga poses that are often held for minutes at a time, Pilates encompasses more fluid movement of the arms and legs using what is called "core strength." This strength comes from the body's torso, from the top of the rib cage to the lower abdomen.

The job of a Pilates instructor is similar to that of a yoga instructor. Pilates instructors also demonstrate and describe motions and check class members' form and technique. Some classes include equipment such as an apparatus called "The Reformer," which is a horizontal framework of straps and strings that is used for over 100 exercises. Class members can tone, build, lengthen, and strengthen muscles by adjusting the equipment's springs to create different levels of resistance.

Both yoga and Pilates instructors have to prepare for their classes ahead of time to choose the exercises and equipment to be used or whether to focus on one method or area of the body. Good instructors are available after class for questions and advice. Instructors should also be open to class suggestions and comments to make the class the best it can be.

REQUIREMENTS

High School
You will need at least a high school diploma to work as a yoga or Pilates instructor. In high school, take anatomy, biology, psychology, and physical education. In addition, get involved in weight lifting, dance, sports, and other activities that will help you to stay fit and learn more about exercise.

Postsecondary Training
Although a college degree isn't always necessary to work in the fitness field, you will be more attractive to employers if your qualifications contain a balance of ability and education. Useful college courses include anatomy, physiology, psychology, kinesiology, biomechanics, chemistry, physics, first aid and safety, health, and nutrition.

Certification or Licensing
Most qualified yoga and Pilates instructors become certified through a professional association, such as the Yoga Alliance or the Pilates Center. For example, the Pilates Center offers a comprehensive program consisting of training on proper form, the purpose of each exercise, how to assess and adjust class members' posture and form, and how to properly pace the class to create an effective and comprehensive class. A certificate is awarded to those who complete a minimum of 96 hours of formal lecture and 750 hours of apprentice work and pass several written and practical tests.

It is important to note that there are no nationally recognized standards for either yoga or Pilates instruction. "Certified" training can be as short as a weekend course or as long as a multi-year program that is the equivalent of a college degree. According to the American Yoga Association, because yoga was historically passed down from teacher to student on an individual basis (creating many varieties and methods), it is unlikely that a standard training program for instruction will be created. Be sure to investigate your yoga or Pilates training program to ensure that it is a quality program.

Other Requirements

Yoga and Pilates instructors are expected to be flexible and physically fit, but they do not have to be in superhuman shape. Though the American Yoga Association has established a list of strict qualities that instructors should adhere to (maintain a vegetarian diet, act ethically), the basic qualities of every good instructor are the same: to be knowledgeable and passionate about your craft and be a patient and thorough instructor.

EXPLORING

The best way to explore these careers is to experience a yoga or Pilates class firsthand. In fact, you should attend several classes to learn the basics of the practice and build your skills. Ask to talk to the instructor after class about his or her job and how to get started. The instructor may recommend a certification program or give you names of other professionals to talk to about the practice.

You may also want to see if a local gym or community center has part-time positions available. Even if you are just working at the front desk, you will be able to see if you enjoy working in a health facility.

EMPLOYERS

Yoga and Pilates instructors work in fitness centers, gymnasiums, spas, dance studios, and community centers. Most employers are for-profit businesses, but some are community-based, such as the YMCA or a family center. Other job possibilities can be found in corporate fitness centers, colleges, nursing homes, hospitals, and resorts. In smaller towns, positions can be found in health care facilities, schools, and community centers.

STARTING OUT

If you have been attending yoga or Pilates classes regularly, ask your instructor for ideas on training programs and if he or she knows of any job leads.

Often, facilities that provide training or internships will hire or provide job assistance to individuals who have completed programs.

Students can also find jobs through classified ads and by applying to health and fitness clubs, YMCAs, YWCAs, community centers, local schools, park districts, religious groups, and other fitness organizations. Many companies now provide fitness facilities to their employees. As a result, students should consider nearby companies for prospective instructor positions.

ADVANCEMENT

Yoga and Pilates instructors who have taught for several years and have the proper training can move into an instructor trainer position or, if they have the needed capital, they may choose to establish their own private studio. To own a yoga or Pilates studio, the instructor should be confident in his or her ability to attract new clients or be willing to ask old clients to move from their old class location to the new studio. With a bachelor's degree in either sports physiology or exercise physiology, instructors can advance to the position of health club director or to teach corporate wellness programs.

EARNINGS

According to the Pilates Method Alliance, Pilates instructors usually charge $10–$30 for group classes and $50–$100 for an hour of personal instruction. CareerBuilder.com reports that yoga instructors who teach in community college extension programs earn an average of $35 per hour. Those who teach in private studios can earn from $30 to $40 per class, with some facilities paying more based on the number of students attending the class. Those who teach in corporate settings can earn $75 an hour or more. CareerBuilder.com reports that, in Los Angeles, successful yoga instructors earn approximately $50,000 per year. The highest profile teachers earn more than $150,000 a year by charging their clients up to $250 an hour.

WORK ENVIRONMENT

Yoga and Pilates classes are generally held indoors, in a studio or quiet room, preferably with a wood floor. Classes can get crowded and hectic at times. Instructors need to keep a level head and maintain a positive personality in order to motivate class participants. They need to lead challenging, yet enjoyable, classes so that members return for more instruction.

OUTLOOK

Health professionals have long recommended daily aerobic exercise and resistance training to maintain weight, build strength, and improve overall health. But more recently, health professionals have added another recommendation: work on flexibility, posture, and stress reduction. These new concerns have given yoga and Pilates a boost in popularity.

The U.S. Department of Labor predicts that the job outlook for fitness instructors should remain very strong over the next several years. As the average age of our population increases, yoga and Pilates instructors will find more opportunities to work with the elderly in retirement homes and assisted-living communities. Large companies and corporations, after realizing the stress reduction benefits of these "softer" forms of exercise, also hire yoga and Pilates instructors to hold classes for their employees.

FOR MORE INFORMATION

For more information about the practice, teaching, and origin of yoga, contact
American Yoga Association
PO Box 19986
Sarasota, FL 34276
Tel: 941-927-4977
http://www.americanyogaassociation.org

Integral Yoga Teachers Association
Route 1, Box 1720
Buckingham, VA 23921
Tel: 434-969-3121, ext. 137
Email: iyta@iyta.org
http://www.iyta.org

For fitness facts and articles, visit IDEA's website.
IDEA: The Health and Fitness Association
6190 Cornerstone Court East, #204
San Diego, CA 92121-3773
Tel: 800-999-4332
Email: nonmemberquestions@ideafit.com
http://www.ideafit.com

For training and certification information, contact
The Pilates Center
4800 Baseline Road, Suite D206

Boulder, CO 80303
Tel: 303-494-3400
Email: info@thepilatescenter.com
http://www.thepilatescenter.com

For information about learning to practice and teach Pilates, contact
Pilates Method Alliance
PO Box 370906
Miami, FL 33137-0906
Tel: 866-573-4945
Email: info@pilatesmethodalliance.org
http://www.pilatesmethodalliance.org

——— INTERVIEW ———

Jim Herbert is a Hatha yoga instructor, program director, and studio owner in Chicago. He was spoke with the editors of Careers in Focus: Coaches & Fitness Professionals *about his job and training background.*

Q. Please briefly describe your primary and secondary job duties.

A. I own and operate a studio, Enso Yoga and Martial Arts, and also teach yoga at a few local health clubs. At Enso, my primary responsibilities include all those that would go into running a small business as well as teaching yoga and martial arts. On a day-to-day basis, I handle bookkeeping, accounting, marketing, recruiting, hiring, cleaning, and anything needed to keep a small business vital and growing. As a yoga teacher, I am constantly studying, practicing, and refining my skills by taking classes with my senior instructors and attending workshops.

Q. Where do you work? Indoors or outdoors? Do you travel for your job?

A. I generally work indoors, although practicing yoga outdoors in the right conditions is a great experience. I spend about 30 hours a week at the studio and also travel to teach at other locations, including other health clubs and private homes. My other travel includes attending workshops both in and out of state and working with a number of private clients in western Michigan where I own a second home.

Q. How did you train for this job? What was your college major?

A. In no way was my college degree related to my yoga instructor training, but many aspects of my studies have helped other aspects of my job. Business skills gained from both education and experience have added to my ability to run a small business. Humanities and Eastern studies classes have helped me to better understand the different approach to health and learning in Eastern practices. Communication studies have allowed me to become more comfortable working with groups of people.

Learning to be a yoga teacher is a study outside of traditional education. It usually consists of an apprenticeship with a senior teacher for a period of a year or two, followed by studies and teacher training workshops. New teachers begin by teaching small beginner classes and slowly expand from there.

Q. How/where did you get your first job in this field? What did you do?

A. I worked hard and was in the right place at the right time to get a break. I had the opportunity to apprentice with one of Chicago's most gifted teachers, Gabriel Halpern, director of the Yoga Circle. I taught his class from time to time when he was on vacation. Eventually, another senior teacher asked me to take over her classes one summer while she was in India on a teaching sabbatical.

Q. What kinds of sources are available to someone looking to get into this field?

A. There are countless opportunities to study and practice the art of teaching yoga. Teacher's conferences occur all over the United States at all times of the year. Most of these events are listed in *Yoga Journal* magazine (http://www.yogajournal.com). The cost of these teacher training programs is generally between $2,000 and $5,000, depending upon the length of the program and the instructors involved. Students can also find work-study and apprentice opportunities with senior teachers. Many large universities, such as the University of Illinois at Chicago, offer yoga as a part if its kinesiology program.

Q. What are the most important personal and professional qualities for yoga teachers?

A. Yoga teachers must love being around people and have a genuine love for making people feel better about themselves. They must also accept the fact that everything they do in their own lives is noticed and measured by their students—lifestyle, attitude, work ethic, practice regimen, diet, etc. The job is an awesome responsibility. Students will see you as a life counselor, motivator, friend, and guru.

You must be organized and able to make a plan for each class and for each student. As a businessperson, you must be able to market yourself and your studios. Since most teachers are paid by "the head," the more people you can recruit to your class, the more money you make.

Q. What are some of the pros and cons of your career?

A. The two best things about teaching yoga are the joy you get from being a positive influence in other people's lives and the fact that you are doing what you love to do every minute of your day.

The cons can be numerous. The work is physically and emotionally demanding. Teaching four or five classes a day requires that you be in great shape and be mentally sharp. Your students' health, well-being, and safety are in your hands every day.

This is not a lucrative job. There are very few teachers that can support themselves or their families just teaching yoga. I would say that a very good teacher who teaches 20 classes a week (a 40-hour per week commitment with travel and preparation) would be lucky to make $30,000 a year. As a result, you have to be prepared to make sacrifices to pursue this path. You will need to work on evenings and weekends and, in all likelihood, you may have to hold another job. Look at my situation for example. I left a corporate job where I worked 50–60 hours a week and made over $80,000 per year. Now I get up at 4:30 in the morning to do my personal practice, teach from 6 to 9 A.M., work in a restaurant 25–30 hours a week, and then go to work at my studio from 5:00 to 9:30 P.M. every day. On weekends, I travel to karate tournaments or teach private lessons. I make about half of what I used to make and I do physically demanding work 70 plus hours per week. I wouldn't trade it for the world, but it is not for the faint of heart. I hear people complaining about how tired they are, or that they had to work 10 hours yesterday, and I think to myself, try my schedule. This must be a labor of love or it just won't work.

Q. What is the most important piece of advice that you have to offer people who are interested in this career?

A. Be prepared to make sacrifices. Listen and learn from senior teachers. Remember that even the most experienced teacher is nothing more than a student and you must maintain that attitude for a lifetime.

When evaluating training programs, note that if it looks too good to be true, it probably is. Any place that suggests that they can certify you to teach yoga in a weekend will make you just that: a teacher with very little knowledge—which is always dangerous. I commend anyone who sets out on the path to teach yoga, but keep in mind that it is a long and tenuous path. I got very lucky. I was in the right place at the right time and had 10 years of previous martial arts teaching experience, which was very applicable to my ability to get jobs and understand the demands of teaching yoga. Most teachers I know spend 10 years trying to make the transition to full-time teacher or have residual income from a related field like massage, dance, etc.

Study the body to learn anatomy. Study Eastern language or history to get a feel how the learning process is different in Eastern studies. Study business so you know how to market yourself and manage yourself as a private corporation. Study any communications field so you learn how to work with group dynamics and be on "stage." Finally, find a great mentor.

Index

Entries and page numbers in **bold** indicate major treatment of a topic.

2001 National Occupational Employment and Wage Estimates 20

A

AAASP. *See* Association for the Advancement of Applied Sports Psychology
AAHPERD. *See* American Alliance for Health, Physical Education, Recreation and Dance
ABCA. *See* American Baseball Coaches Association
ACE. *See* American Council on Exercise
ACSM. *See* American College of Sports Medicine
activities coordinators (recreational therapists) 124
ADA. *See* American Dietetic Association
adapted physical education teachers 102
Adidas 13
administrative dietitians 48
aerobics 4–6
Aerobics and Fitness Association of America (AFAA)
  certification 8, 12, 72
  contact information 11, 63
  information source 13, 61
aerobics instructors 4–14
AFAA. *See* Aerobics and Fitness Association of America
AFPA. *See* American Fitness Professionals and Associates
AMA. *See* American Medical Association
American Alliance for Health, Physical Education, Recreation and Dance (AAHPERD)
  contact information 32, 108, 119, 140
  continuing education programs 125
  student membership 105
American Association for Leisure and Recreation 129
American Baseball Coaches Association (ABCA) 32, 140
American Board for Certification of Teacher Excellence 104, 108
American College of Sports Medicine (ACSM)
  certification 8, 13
  contact information 11, 152, 170
  guidelines established by 12
American Council on Exercise (ACE)
  certification 8, 13, 37, 60, 92
  contact information 11, 41, 63, 70, 95
  employment 38
  source data 97

American Dietetic Association (ADA)
  certification 52
  Commission on Dietetic Registration 52, 57
  contact information 41, 56
  earnings data 55
  employer 38
American Federation of Teachers 107, 108
American Fitness Professionals and Associates (AFPA)
  certification 37, 60, 92
  contact information 41, 63, 96
American Football Coaches Association 32
American Hockey Coaches Association 32
American Medical Association (AMA) 152, 164
American Orthopedic Society for Sports Medicine 152
American Psychological Association (APA) 155, 156, 157, 158, 162
American Red Cross 77, 79, 80
American School Health Association 108
American Society for Nutritional Sciences (ASNS) 41, 56
American Society of Association Executives 87
American Society of Exercise Physiology 62
American Speakers Bureau Corporation 86, 87
American Therapeutic Recreation Association 125, 129, 132
American Yoga Association 172, 173, 178
Amherst College 99
APA. *See* American Psychological Association
apprenticeship programs 9
aquatics manager 79
aquatic specialists 79
Aristotle 142, 163
Arizona 64
Arizona Diamondbacks 144
Arizona State University 144
art therapists 122
arthroscopic surgery 144
asanas 172
Ashtanga Yoga 173
ASNS. *See* American Society for Nutritional Sciences
assistant coaches 113
Association for Education in Journalism and Mass Communication 42
Association for the Advancement of Applied Sports Psychology (AAASP) 157, 158, 162
Association of Tennis Professionals 120
Athens, Ohio 18
athletic administrators 15
athletic directors 15–24